A Book – By Riley Parker Miller

A Book – By Riley Parker Miller

"A New Beginning In The New World Order Part III"

"My War's Willing, And Then Totaled Life"

The Story Of War By The Impersonator
of the World Leading Office of US
President, During The Third World War

"A New Beginning In The New World
Order Part III"

By – Riley Miller

Words Spoken In Tongues By
The Holy Ghost, And Decided On
By My God's All-Knowing Teaching,
And Omnipresent Prophesy Of Powerful
Language Meanings

"My War's Willing And Then Totaled Life"

(Written Truest From The Top Order of the Bear, As Its National Symbol; From World War Three)

By: Riley Parker Miller

(A Death's – Allied Construction Book)

The Book Was Written On Friday,
September 25, 2015, The Date Of My
New Life!

I am a President, Of America's War –
"World War 3!

" The New World Order Is The
Secretive Life"

There is a secret, only one in every
millions, of people, has ever heard of!
Its message, is so secretive that only one
of these one, in every millions, of
people, can even know about; it! The
demands, from its hands are so very
subtle, that only one or one is fifth of the
fractions, of the percentages of soldiers
marching, ever goes; into what is in it!!
The secret remains alive, in history's
times, about secretive life.

It is the one and only, real secret! In our
worlds, one and only, a few to a single
few, at every institution, in each world;
can even, of can in living ever heard of
it; most have all, died off! In, all of this
world, and all over the world, and of
worldwide publications, one and only –
one voice; as can ever heard of it; and
keep quiet, with not going – insane.
Over, the marches of time, no one can
keep their mouths, closed about it! It is
the reason why the US Presidents, are
shot! It is in the "New World Order!!"

The "One World Government" Of
Americans

The persons, involved in the war of the
third world war. The government, has
its employees. The good of
government's works, and the state, have
the church, and the religion, from
himself, in Christ! The third wave, of
death, is World War, from Three Times!
The third, world leader, is me! I, as
myself am guided to, and by the
Antichrist?

Due, to the Biblical Revelations, I think
that he, is real. The deals, from the New
World Order! I, win, due to the
Antichrist? Christians over the entire
world war three, are played by the
Antichrist.

Our Founding Fathers must have made
an oath. They, all created, the US
Government. The, laws are of, his. The
future, is from the US Constitution,
wins. The document ""let us go", is
based of the lands, in the laws.

The living ways, of World War Three,
are triple fold, mine. The governments,
overnight, will form. The war's people,
will be impressed!!

The soldiers; in wars! The – fight from
the freedom of America. The soldiers;
in America always, win. The "One-
World Government," will happen, as an
overnight, Illuminati, surprise!

The plans, for the night. The N.W.O.
third one-world; "government"? The
future, is mine! The oaths, of the office.
The "Office of the United States'
President!"

The War Of World Wars, Of Three!" –
The Antichrist

There is a "World War Three!!" I, can
win, this war. It, must, become its own,
the thinking of the "Superpowers". To
start, what is world war three, there must
be victims.

The superhuman race is of the
Antichrist. The laws and its deeds, are
Constitution from, its based legal

signings. God's laws! The World of
Three Wars, is the United States going
on, to war!

The American legal system. The laws,
and your goals, are all from
Constitutional legality, from the new
age. The "Antichrist Age;" is already,
lost and gone forever. The Antichrist,
America is one man?

The values, of human strength, in
characters. The lands of the superhuman
forces, from the Antichrist? Now, we
are in the Trinity, of the "Third World
War"!

These meanings from the wars, are then
anarchy, and annihilation. The Third
World War's humanity, begins now.
But, the Illuminati, powers it, as all!

The American tradition loses, unless we
won, all wars. The not at hand, is the
lost. The war is not lost, of World War
Three!

America, has always won; these three
wars!

The Titles, From The President Over
The Office Of War, In The United States
of America; For the One World
Government, World War Three, And
The, "New World Order!"

I, Will Become Willed, In This Life As
The "One Voice". From The Past
Spoken Words From War, Of World
Leaders.

In The History Of Wars, From the
Present In The New Age to the
President, and the Future, From the
Willing, and Then Totaled Life!

I, have won! The world, is a leadership
life. Wrote, of agreements. I, fated an
agreement. The world, of designs. I
will, to live! I see in the faces of war!
Eyes, seeing all, in this world.

I Can Live! In My War's, Life! The
Battled, Head of Numbered Lives! I,
Chose Liberty! I, from the war of the
worlds, wins. Nobody wills, the chosen
President!

As My Writing Book, Language! I
wrote one-hundred books. My life, is
not the best agenda. The writings are

done in time. The places, names, and
times, are mine. The books, are in the
shelves. This books, message is in the
totality, in the wars.

This Book Is Dedicated To My Life –

To – My Family and Friends; In My Life
To – HIS Bridgebuilders; Of Dallas
Ministry
To – Young Life; In New York
To – The Wynne Family; From Texas

The War Things That Can And Do Make
Sense

I Wrote This Book –

– "My War's Willing and Then Totaled
Life"

- By : Riley Miller

Politics Around the Entire World

The Americans, We Know; Who Have
To Win, The –
"World War Three"! This is, what world
war is third!

If, I Supported The Argument, That
America, In "The New World Order;" Is
Solid! My Bid, Is For President!

In The Wars For Those Dedicated To
The War's Sold Souls From The Past
Lives; To The End.

The Temptation, Is From Wars To Wins
– To The Book Of Life!!!

The Lamb, Is Agreed!! The history on
these books, are of the world, and is
agreed, within, the world's top, World
War Three", position and superpower,
super roles! I, am in a Napoleonic age,
of power structures, that I, cannot ever
try, to change; as my America, is
climaxing, as the global elite, is reaching
its end.

The Faithful and Fatefully True Is
Ending And False Is Beginning, Is
Nothing As In This Nomination For
President Goes To – The Man Who Is Of
The Represented Placement of Texas!

Who Votes For: "Riley Miller"?! The
American People!

Alive; For Warring Office Of The
United States of American's, First Off
Wynne Family Of Texas, Forming Me,
And My – U.S.A. President!

All of the USA; Of The Finest Texan
Families!! The Deals, Are Done! The
Texas, New World Order; Is
Demonstrated!

Who, brought all, of the books and
written hits home, to the American
family, from the man in charge, of social
gain? Ask, my family!

A War Bird's Song –

As Is In Life Is As In Death! World War
3 Will Begin – And The USA'S
President's; Will Be Of WW3! (As Its
All-Time Leader)

The War's Book The Authentic Work
By Riley Miller
Guaranteed; of True Authentication of
Work and True Authorship Of Mine!

I, Riley Miller, have truly agreed, and
accurately measured, a new life.
Thousands, of words, I do know solely,
in having to, have to wrote this book. I
am the one who has admitted guilt, for
written the entire work, from the
writings, of the entire mine, of the world.
The work is a work of art, treasured by
other men and women, of war books.
The fiction and world, is in the unknown
and fictional warred times, of the
entrance into, the three parts, to –
"World War Three!"

I, have agreed and confirmed, is that I,
am a true soldier. In, this book is,
Heaven's honorable mention.

From this book, is for the American
people, of the masses, and from the
masses, of the American people. In
these times, we shall win freedom, the
working minds, in the entrance into the

halls of fames; towards the superpowers, of world war three's Nuclear Weapons. The prose, and the poetry from my words, come out alive, and in the mind, of this book! To send away, a present, and into the lives of the American publics, comes my alone, bid for the Untied States of American Presidency, from the current President Barrack Hussein Obama!

"Just a hand in the bush"! People know, I am of this war book; of this versed word quality, and in the meant realism. In, this life, from the sole works of me, and only of me, my inheritance is in this book; and is written in words by – Riley Parker Miller!

The Warnings and Cautions of the Book, In The Formative Knowledge; For the Reader:

The cautions of the message are of the words and meanings, contents. The author's words formed, as are the written words, for a meaning from the book's valuable message. The continents in its message, warns of the message, from

how the book; is in its – "WW3"! The
whole book, revolves around the world.

I have acknowledged, prose and
philosophy, to the reader, and as in that I
noticed, that I have been from myself, in
this writing, as in what is; "My Life"!

Myself; Riley Miller, is the author, and
its book's messages, as the sole author,
and the bond originator, of this book is;
the new message! In the book's
complete circle, of life is the message,
on "wars"!

In the book's written authority; and in
my authorship, for in my real name, and
I am the sole penned authorship, of this
book!

My value, of authorship, approved is in
the name of – *Riley Miller*!

My written book, and the penned works,
of myself; I, am a really, known writer,
in works of; myself!

I have admitted true, and in the writings,
of this book's authenticity from myself,

as the writer; in the evidence of this book!

The book is admitted solely, to be written by me, and in this; authorship of this phenomena, is the book, by – <u>Riley Parker Miller!</u>

The author, for taken a meaning from the book, and its warning messages, have warned of the book's message! I, arrived the book's message, from the title of the, "book!" I have in reading, acknowledged, that one is to the reader, that I, Riley Miller, am the author, and of this, am the sole author, and originator, in this – book!

In this book's write, and in solely, my named authorship, for in my penned name, I am the sole author, of this book. I am Riley Parker Miller!

My Authorship, by *Riley Miller.*

All, of this book's contents, and are true and false situations, and/or real and, imagined persons, and the works, in any books, and/or written works, of mine, are solely from; Riley Miller!

All these writings are all guaranteed, as
the true and sole works, from the books;
of "me."

In my penned writings, as in my
approved works, and in my guaranteed
work, is by my authorship, as guaranteed
to become, greatness in writing, from the
penmanship – of the one man's, penned
writing, from a lie from myself.

The War's Book!

In Sentence Warning –

This book has a cautionary message, to
all readers, of the words, the titles, and
the phrases, that can be of offense, to
other writers.

In, taking aim, to please the readers. I,
have in no place, claimed as my life, in
terms, as what are of the events, made of
this book that can enter the reader. The
reader digression, and the author
pervasive worded vocation, will be
advised.

The book, from warring contents, of the
certain words and phrases in battles, and
in the knowledge, in this book, therein
can be explicit knowledge, in the book.
The warnings is for the reader, to be
very warned, while from the explicit
meanings, that is in the intelligence, then
the writer alone, only in his language,
shall he excels.

There is not a new world order, in the
writings of this book. The fictional
events and, true persons, and the same
factual world, comes in the writing

world, as of this book, spoken is in terms
for the readers, as in "true"!

To note in the language and in him the
penmanship, from the general ideas,
there are certain judgments, in this book
that should be used, in the book
message.

Warning of the book, that is of powerful
words, and the elicit content of the
expressed ideas; as is of "philosophy"!

As in writing stories, the American
Public Office has to be used by, the
mind of each reader. Explained, then the
teacher known as itself, to become as; is
to be – "Jesus Christ!"

All goes out, to the warnings of the book
to the reader, is a cautionary crucifixion
content of caution, from the ideas and
the meanings, of the book, to the public,
of the reborn, "President of the USA!"

The Book's Cautionary Message –

The writer's written work, has advised
caution, in a warning to the reader, from
the author. The warnings, is for the

book readers. This is to stay, aware of, this book, and its contents, while reading man.

The book's message, is the content meaning, as expressed as in the book in; "the content warning!"

The works, which is what comes in meaning, and is issued meanings of the words, and in its expressions, therein is, "Intelligent War!" I, am not sure, of the meaning, of the President of the United States!

In books, wars are as to be, forewarned! My books, to that in what he wrote, is written from myself; "Riley Miller"! I, in knowledge as from the self, and as of myself, as to what are for the writings, published by me. That words are from himself, as the works from the author; myself of, Riley Parker Miller. I, am the one author, of this book, in its – War Order.

To know and learn, in whom is the fact-based written worker, who in writing commencing "in-person", is in the author; of "Riley Parker Miller!" In

writing, one holds the history, of wars,
by writing in this book!

While the readers can, use the caution
from whom is the writer; that is the
author, and as are his warnings, voiced
from himself!

Riley Miller and only Riley Miller, can
express himself; on written books, from
his own! Pat, of the new world order
began as history's works, as himself of a
writing book! Good will be to, all in a
noble man's, good renown name! For, a
good name, is to be valued higher, than
any of the world from – The Rich!

My caution, is in means and implicated,
knowledge – which is power. The words
and intelligence, is of the open heart.

The open heart as a circled organ from
life, made true as in opposing sides, of
the intellect from humanity, and in the
ending, of the human races; comes what
is known, the wars!

The source, is for the warless nations,
and from all inactions for our nations.
Tried and true America, which we, all
win itself, on wartime wars.

What sides are from just cause, that
which are on all of its sides; in world
wars! The winning, of American's
stolen wars, on the American sides;
comes as an absent-minded professor, to
his student!!

The land is property, that is won over, by
the masses of the knowledge, of man!
The conservation of the dollar! The
sign, of the times. The lacks, of
education! The success; on the face of
the dollar bills!

Deciding and depending on their sides, if
on the sides of the book of this war of
Americanism, it is declared as the starter
book for, "World War Three!" I can
think of new world order, from the
writing warnings that can merely
happen; as to be what are from the
provisions, from the interests of man.

Intellect and reason, about war things!
Intellect and reason, from peace from
America. Born into , the America! As,
a true Texan family's inheritors, I can
outdo, from the authored works; in many
writings from wars.

The named and namely history, for all
works and not known of all from these
names, **after** worded meaning's sides,
and are winning values! The certain, are
for the explicit; safety? In the wars,
from our countries!

The American lands and property of an
American nations, from laws and
protections; wins wars! The good name,
is of good implicit substance, in the
desired image of a person, of the
resounded the names! Must, be Wars!
The wars, is in an American national
substantial movement.

The book has these warnings, and given
us therein a caution, to work, as the
advisory noticed, of here, in the book,
and, this author's meanings, from the
book's – "valued message"!

From the good and greatest, names are to
become valued – by "The God From
Good"!

The author of – "My War's Willingness
And Totaled Life," is me! I, am –
"Riley Miller"!

I, will add words, into this book context,
as a ritual, to write, the very best books,
in the best stores, libraries, and on the
walls, of the greatest people's, lives in –
"The Church!"

From The Author's Desk – To The
Reader's Book On His Laptop
Computer, In The Kitchen On The
Table, Or In Line For War!

The True World Knows

The notice, of the advisory, in what is in
strong topics, and the highest meanings,
ever intended. The reader, should read
this book.

The warning of the topics of the book,
are real and true, from the knowledge, in
the intended and from the used, life of
the author!

The words, are the author's voice, and
his own used words, are not, and is not,
from the intellect and from the reasoned
mind – known to be true or false.

And, in supportive knowledge of
authorship, and the minded words of
readers, are from the, substance and
intelligence, of the mind – for both
reader, and in the author, alike!

In reading the book, the author endorsed
all, as in the reader's judgments,
everything to be judged, as "Parental
Advisory"!

Riley Miller, is the author in the book,
"My War's Willing And Totaled Life."

The topic and plot, of what is in the
followed idea, and in an supporting
caution in words of expression, we
approach the ideas, with what and, with
the book's contents! Myself, as an
available reader, should be very
forewarned, that intellect's – the book's
warning, be very advised.

The warnings, are for the explored
meaning, and to the approach, is true for
every reader. Due, in the topics and in
the active intent, on the reader, is to
address the reader. The read and known
intents, from the book, is a general
consent warning, for what meanings of
words are intentioned to be, and the
meanings of language means, the book
really is mine. The contents, and the
official and explicit, meaning, adhere
from the book warning.

The title of the book, as in an introduced
idea and a new kind of topic, in the
knowledge and the expression. The
wages of sin, from the words of the
father, of this book, is a "new writing
attempt"!
As a writer, on the intent of meaning,
intelligence is from, the pages of the
book. Therefore to the reader, and from

a topic explained, be cautioned of the
content in the book.

The book is of a warning of words.
Messages and contents, of people,
places, and things, is based from the
ideas in the present time, person, date,
and place.

The idea and knowledge are warned to
the readers, as measurements of the
people, places, and times. In usage of
the words, names, and the locations, is in
an age, and time, and in a date's places.

The book's write of words, and in its
contents, are from the mind of the
author. This is a warning in the context.

The meaning usage and used
paraphrased ideas, is from the
impressions, of a new idea, of the world.
In the words, from the content, and ideas
from the reader, as in newfound ideas
can be expressed.

The author impress, to the mind of the
reader, a new topic. The author shows
the reading audience, the intentions from
the pages and the words, to be warned of
write language, in age and time, of

warnings, due to the main impression of the theme.

The book message is for the age, of readers. The author, in his ways, means, and topics; is that he made up all of the ideas. True to his topics, he paged the book's message, as a book wrote down, the authored and penned, of writing of himself. The written book's central message.

The author wrote down and expressed himself in, the theme, and language, and idea, his topic. He, supported the new wrote, from form, page, sentence, and language, the life of a new reader.

Thanks, to the book's message, for the reader; I am Riley Parker Miller

To know and to go enter, into my world!
Welcome readers, to the war of world
for the third time, and killings place. I,
given a choice, of to go forth, and enter
to a mighty plan. Or, to not read, and be
of my own construction. In the enter, to
war. And the exit, to peace. Choices
from mine, are as I, in the doings of war,
or from peace.

Riley Miller, gives the reader the
choices, of a life or a war, of what is in a
life planned or, a failed life, with only,
you and me!

Come with me, on a written plan, of
fulfilling prophesy. The book, is your
manual, and true life, is what, you can
expect. The life, and the death, of the
modern-day man.

The Author's Message – How To Know
The Language

The War's Messages For The American
Presidency

The book's author, is new. He, had a
new branded impression, on the reader.
From a Idealistic, Book's Message!

The codex, from world war three's
inevitability. I, do so and can think, of
that which I, can write, with, in the new
world order. For the new world order
run, and fully operated wars! From, the
worlds! By my stance, of mine in an
age, of – "Wars"!

By the knowledge used, of the author,
there is a readable warning. There is a
message, and a contented use, of
important – The President's Ideas!

The Ideas Onto Usage, And Into
Dangerous Themes, Why The Presidents
Can Be Warned Of, Into The Scores Of
The Ways From The Futile, And The
Most Holy Ways, Of The Most Holy
God – Of, "My Life And Fortune"!

The Wars, Of America Over Wins, The

America Author's Thoughts. How He Wrote in the Meaning of Words, and of the Explicit Ideas!

The Warning of Themes of Wars, In Philosophy, Wherein I Can Be Seen, In American Democratic Implications and, In War's!

I Have The American Dreams, From The American War's Times, And the Top Of The Expressions Of Greatest Intentions, To Lead This Country, Into The Shores, Of World War Three, and Cross To The Other Land, For Safety! The Three World Wars; In The Presidents; That Are Inside Of Us, Are As Americans! The Truth, Shall Set Us All Free!

As Worlds, Are Eventually Evenly Words And Made, Not War-Based, If I Ask Of In Caution of The Terms, In Titled Plans, Demonstrated By Fact, of the Knowledge, In the Messaged – "The Holy Bible!

When Reading This Book, The Reader Must Be Of Legal Age, And In Legal Ability To Read, For The Rights, To Bear.

The ability to become the one of the
Presidency of the United States, can and
wills, to the come, of the Americans, to
the American Presidency. The United
States way, is to God!

The Book's Notable Warnings Of
Existentialism, Can Cause The Reader,
Of What Is My Only, Concern, In What
Is For The Reader, To Be Of That, What
Is From Mentioning God's Church,
From Christ's Messaged Ends! Christ's
Prophetical "World of Warring Times!!"

All Of This Book, Is Asked To Be
Explained Herein, In These Great War's
Book Messaged Lifeblood! Onto,
History's Pages Bled Blood Over All Of
The Presidential Office Of War's Deaths
and Lives; Covered All Of Americans,
From the Times And Living Spaces, To
The USA Of America's Presidential
War, Of The USA's Presidency – Three
Worldwide Wars, Are On The Book Of
Life!

It, Is Intelligence, And Then It, Is Up To
The Third Time, As Citizenship Of The
United States of America, In The Third

Order From The American Warring;
Futures!

But, As In Now, The World Peoples
Warring Lead Role As Its Head Of
American War Office; As A Third War's
Office Of The USA President; Fighting
All of the American Leading Roles Of –
"A One World Order!"

A Fight For, "The One World
Government!" In Fighting, In Sides for
the, "American World War Three!" A
War For The, "Illuminati of the
Internet!" The Winning War For The –
"God Of Church!" The War's Words
On Wars Waged of, "If not only
American, What Else Is There – "The
Ends Wins Of God??!!"

A World War Three – Office Of The
USA Presidency! The Ballot Votes, Are
Simply What Are, Undermined By The
American Public's Voting Systematic
Presenting!

The Followings of the American
Witness of Wars And The Missionary
For Peace, Therein Is The Side Winning
Of Wars, Therein Located What Is Of
the Man From History's Wars, Who –

"Dated Destruction!?

The President of the USA, In Who
Excels In The America's Third World
War; Is The Antichrist!

To, The Trusted Followings From Him,
And Into This American Sadness And
Elected History Of Wars, Measured
Costliness, Counts In Morality, and
Starry-Eyed Images, From The Words,
Which May Cause In War's Harmed
Living, The Desire Of War States To
The Mind!

The Book's Demand For A War Title -

In Makings Of "World Wars" From The
Costs, Of This Life To The Riches Of
Mine, In American Lands, Americans In
Made Out Of The General Warnings, Of
World War That Is Coming, In
Americanism In Spreading Wars – The
War To End All Wars!

To The Head of the Office of the
President of America and The World –
World War Three Is Coming! The Third
World War Is Coming!

The Beware of the End of the World –

The World War Three Is Coming!

By: Riley Parker Miller

To The Reader's Best Interest, A War
Manual, On The Book As Is The
Explained In the Explained Topics, –
Made From Myself, As If I May Ask Of
Others, To Be Of The Presidents, Until
To Third Coming of The Antichrist
World Wars. Make Notice Of, And in
the USA Plan, To Obey the President of
the USA's; Dammed Choice!

The Choices, In America, Are Dying
Off, As the Opportunity Costs, Of An
World Of Wealth, Enter Is the Worldly!

In My Life, As Are in Lives from the
Three World's Wars – If, You Are
Forewarned, To Reading This Book!!!! –
May, Living Life's, Happiness Cannot
Come True, Unto Yourself, In Life!!
The Losing Battles of Everyday Life, Is
Never Ending, In Life's Cultured And
Obsolete, Endings of the Battle, Even In
Just Going, To Get A Tank, Of Gas.

Into Seeing My Themed Writing's
Scenarios, I've Warned the Book's
Readers, In the Intellects of the Book

Topics, Inside Of What Has Everyone
Of War's Wins – We, Are Following the
USA's World Third Wars, And In,
Returning To War, And Then Tuning In
To The, "World War Three!" Riley
Miller Has The Wins Over – "The
President Of The USA!" The War's
God's Trinity, In Himself He Is Who
You Are Thinks, How He's Alive From
All Omni's, Of Him; And Of The New
World Order; In Good Doesn't Come;
Unless Good, Of The Ages, Of Itself!
The Come, Fall Life From God, The
One From – Blessed As The Good And
Faithful – God!

The Healing From The Truth Of The
Nations, Will Come, From the Turning
Around, In The Good, of God!! Even, If
The Nations Of The Healing, Does Not
Come? If God and His Good, Doesn't
Come?! Even If, The God, The One
Who Prevails Over The Good, And In
The Healing, And Is There Any Good;
Then We Begin Already For Battle! The
Healing Of The Nations; I Declare In
God's Good, Does Not Come, Then
Does Come; Based In God! The Good
Is Basic And Fundament, Of Healing In
Our God; For Everything Under The
Sun!!!

As In History Of American Wars –
From The War Of America's National
Free World, Politics, At A Call Of Duty,
Inside From the Followings of Antichrist
America's World War Three; Arrived
The Messages From One Office Of
America Peopled Mass Certainly
Agreed, On American Wars In Sold,
Ancient Aged, Times Of The New
World Order!

The Decided Voting War Office From
The Pen In The Hand Of One Man, The
Presidents of the United States of
American, President's Office! When
Killings, Of What Majority Rules For
Me Won Are, In To The Future
Presidential Positioned Lifestyle, From
the Voted American Party of Republican
By The Elected Idea, To His Matters to
Win Over All Of My USA War Office -
In "World War Three!"

Final Home In Book Writing, Is On
Books On The Laws, Of Wars, My War
Office, My US Lead Role, As Everyone
As All, Learned From The Powers Of
My Desk!

Everything, For The New World Order, is an wartime's USA Electoral Leader, from a Presidency, for an Office, and Trials of Freedom, and Tribulations of Popular Votes, Caste as Ballots, and Consented As The of the American Leader, of Freedom, Democracy, and in Life! The laws of the land, are before time, place, and life, and can be what, bring me into power, by the will of the lands.

The able citizens from laws, high marked above, ourselves, is a New World Order, from lands, and the laws. Hand in hand, the willing powers for a freedom, should triumph, during the war, of the World War Three! In the Wisdoms of USA's President of America, Of Publicly Decided American Work, I Will, A Third World War. I Will What Are In Everyone's Americans, Must Be Cautious, To The Book's Working Parties, And Past Warring States, And, America's 'New World Order – Of The Republican Party of Texas! Lives, From True Idealism, From American Presidential, Public and Private, USA Elected Officials, Disown Their Rags, And Fully Fund The World War Three's Times!

The words, "alive," and, "dead," are
truly meaningful words. Alive, in
truthfulness, and honesty, in covering
three world's wars, how humans exist
are from meanings, of life and death. To
die freely, is however we all end, and to
end by decided choosing life, and for to
live, is by wars. Both signals of lost or
won doors, won and opened into
freedoms, because making beloved the
unloved, and unlivable persons in "world
war three", is now the stage set, from the
– "American Free World Leader!!"

America, has three duties in this life,
and, in three sides of the Triangle, there
are three numbers. One of its sides does
what makes the past's world war, from
the ages of the costs, of the worldly
wars.

The two or twice-sided nickel, wins the
war, in three-sixes. To all numbers, in
the take-over, Omega's of sided coined
meanings, the "Tripled-Six," is cometh
from the – "New World Order!" The
second winning's sides, of the double-
edged coin, wins world wars, at the third
world war's flopped side, and is into the

saving of the lost souls, Heaven's
Americans, are in the measured of the
peace, of the immediate present, of
peace's! And third or threefold coined
flipped, comes out of the shadows, the
natural World War Three, and how
America wins, overall of these wins over
all! The collections from world war
three's madmen; collected dusted
jackets, from the aged, and golden
books!

Americans of the all races, creeds, and
religions, do winning sides, to cover all
over, the entire world's identity, of the
entirety of wars! One is for lost and
found peoples; and another as, from
winning sides, from American sacred
nations. We sing songs, as forward as it,
into the foundations, of my United States
future's life, of what are exemplified
inside the war lines. To make a golden
and solid statement, the plans enter into
the American soldier's outcome plans, in
the USA, single handedly winning and
losing, everyone's wars, and each and
all, Presidential sides wars!

The new world order, as the American
dream, is the warning from the only

sidedness, from the one homestead, as an, "American Dream!"

The "dream of Americans." to the sold nationalists, are of living homesteads. In American home's soil, as invested, from what are merely with, "one man;" is not how the American dream, is; as taken place!

Not or nothing, to the Antichrist from American worldly lives, is going onto, whatever seas, who defeat the sailor, from wars, in the – "The American President!"

The three old-aged wars, of war times, are from America's wartimes. In foundations, where there exists, a living and breathing, action of good people – what are the costs?

Wars, in this USA freedom's lands, are from time spent, counting the days until we are freed, as a national people. Life or the living sides, and from dead and the not the alive sides, of the American people, consistently wanted to be in dealt deals of the wars in basically, "made-to-win" – "wars!" The made-

man, from World War Three; is the
Antichrist man.

In the wars, of the decided American
viewpoints, itself in the reason and
ourselves, in the meanings, is what
comes; from all-around. Is, what I
intend, on giving? In itself am I in
wealth, of what are three sides in the
world wars, of the sided worlds of,
America's?! In the United States war,
that won the wars, over killing the
Antichrist, and in ending the American,
costs in the inner lives; on lives is Riley
Parker Miller!

The enemy always, is not, the one; who
plots. The enemy countries, from wars
did cover and move all together, as a
plot around the world in what, is
consisting of warring places! In Holy
Bibles, in around all, of the globe;
missionaries. The places of war that the
nemesis hit, is in warring ways of the
American's innocent souls, whose won
the global, elected' vote. The majority
vote, is mine, from the USA Presidency!

Twins, from conjoined diamonds, one
for these sellable profits, and in the other
plots, in the alive profits, accumulated

the remained sums! To money, of the
profiting money; is wars. Wars in the
mind of billions, gain to the wealthy
status, from the natural invested
resources, in the costs, and from the
profits in gains, of the sellable men and
women, of World War Three!

Money comes of gaining resources, as
natural man, and powerful forces of
actions, priced out in theirs of interest,
from Billions of Dollars in banking
counted, on gross natural resources. The
person of wealth, or the man in demand
of gaining finances, will someday in
gain of ourselves in gaining resources,
for the start of three wars, from the
killing off of innocent people, to the
enemy soldiers, that coming home, love
the lands, and its laws. They were used
to dying, from its laws.

Wars are started in order to advance in
goods and services, all along the road to
success, and heal the blind man, into the
freedom of the world. Eventual winning
sides can altogether make sizing
planning strategy, to anyone's gain –
"War of Three Worlds." Ask anybody,
if a reader of this book, if we are what,
has a Doomsday device hidden and

buried in the doorway's entryway, on the
lands of golden streets, and branded
currency; of hard-workers, and motives
for accumulation of, all-possible,
consists from the wealth, from the
accumulated American world wars.
Wars are alike in this messaged of
meaningful virtues, of the lives paid at
that, of what are at the expense to the
owner. The "Promised Lands", of the
American warring lands, are made in the
plans of the – new world order, of the
currency, of the USA's measured
wealth, as in the currency of the
American dollar bill.

(How the USA Is About Winning) - (All
Of The American's World War Three's,
Truest Times, But Is In The Presidential
Terms; One Presidential Office, Comes
From WW3!)

Masses, of wartimes of peopled masses,
ordered from the fall of man as killed,
and as extinction, in the idealisms of
dead persons, from all of the centrifugal
knowing terrorist plots, that always aim
to, scared Americans.

If, their approaches mask, of the war's
fighting aged lifestyle, is supposed to
kill off, enemy's lands. Off of itself, of
wars, from our USA friend, or allied
forces of countries, waged wars and
signed peace, are of penned signature at
world wars! As, living life has opened
up closed doors, a third America comes
wise and intelligent, as the suitably put
ideas, to the forms of life, inside of the
word, idea, sentence, "war," and the
phrased words, "world peace!"

To the endings of the past earth, as
"living and dying," and to the new
beginnings of the new lands on earth, of
the living and dying dreams; spur on the
warring times. Covering of the globe,
all over the world, muscular wins, are
with togetherness in sided forces, as onto
front languages, are from supportive
people.

Approach and deeming acceptance, a
new war history's walk on sandals, on
both sides, of the Earth, is then flipped
the nickel, as the American coin's; side
in three's from coin sided tossed, from
as a win, – "Three World Wars!!"

Wars, unless in caused reasoning from all deaths, in not one, but not even just one man, in sized hands can cover the "Tree of Life," and our mistakes. To uncover the hands, of time in war's funding, is to pay all of the world's war's, arming and armed forces, in anybody's mother, and her brother, the sums of millions of dollars, in costs. In dollars of spending from collected spending costs, the USA's, military warfare, costs surpluses of billions of dollars, in overhead spending. In wars then natural resources, moves in foreign lives, and can end wars by negating the valuable, dollars. But, why I am willingly accepting life, as the truest, medical doctor role played by the American President, who seeks outs wins, will cause wars!!

The world war, from made-up times and, in the examples from this life, as in my greater life, I win, the President's position. To stand on America's soil, wind down on a hot cup of hot cocoa, and sit down by the home fire, then American as I am, I can then watch, television. Marked in, warfare and nihilism, humanity lost, not in wars of non-existing, but in lost wars, that are existing plans, with murderous enemies.

Surrender to the real living lives, from my USA in leadership role, into the Presidential terms, of the willingness, to win. World wars, came from the officers of the USA wartimes, costing what war is to costs, and coming from what in wars, not ever came from what is not, in wartimes!

Planning wars, in what is having coming plans, means all things in the world, to what it is, to have the leadership role. Standing up, into the war leadership role as followings, for all American wins; is the child. He, stands up, there in what is from a standoff, of peace and love, and killing and war! He believes in the good from other children, playing in sands, from the wars, we need to generate the national economy! To protect the USA's children, then we need wars from foreign lands. To stimulate the warring economy; winning frontlines go further, forthcoming in entering into the war ring's costs, and from the sizeable table, the cold costs from the entire wars and, then in the wartimes, allowed of that, costs of sizable money!"

In wars, and times in what are real wars;
meaning occurs inside of books. This
outward story, is at novel tales, making
whose life is, written from what is – war.
The message and words, about the book,
wrote down in living, and dead life,
dwell within the sands, of time. The
history of, the literature work, was
expressed in the pages, as of old you
opened, designed within parts, desired
good; in deals. History's paged written
exampled and open-minded opened
ancient pages that are in these contextual
analyses well enough are made of
agendas, as sold, aged olden wars.

An 'New Time Order' sees America
history, as if what are extinct thoughts of
war, are opened to the paged, meant
ideas, that happen after numbered and as
is, as the warring manuals. Islands, as
in, opened lands, exists as if are
meanings, in unnecessary warring
agreements, from long, long ages ago,
then killing intellectually is made, in
offers, then in wars ages, gone in the
past. The documents of the pastimes
from wars in America still are being
analyzed in standard, wars from that
what is, used, from foreign warring

countries!!! Over, and over, again and
once again, the aged "new world order,"
of the American one man's history
pages, are documented; in this world
war! In this life's, war's humankind,
three wars occurring are from six kings,
of the world of wars, from history as in,
previous and existing, document's
warred; writing pages!!

The knowledge, of the beast, and
antichrist, are of one man; or the triple-
six, marked on the hand, and forehead.

The history, as war's pages, of past
fights by, the sword, of world wars of
the third kind, in measures of the
intellect, as in the reader, and as in his
mind, do exist. Therein wars, of war and
world war three, warnings. The words,
and ideas, are of the readers, as
portrayed by explicit age levels, warned
of in, the book, in a certainness, of
accurate information, or in the followed
fashion, of if incidents, people, or places,
are directly, as a spoken words known
as, "accurate" or "true." If, there is a
warning for the book, and in how the
words, and meaning of the messages,
can be portrayed; it is for others of
reading knowledge, to the book be the

readers, as if hurtful, fatalist, or, decreed,
in and as the same discretion, as if being
warned, by an authority, for accurate
tales, and not truthfully portrayed,
readerships' events! All people in all
situations are not, to do with literal
interpretation of every word and phrase,
in this book's meaning on truthful,
occasions. If, in prophesy written
purposes, of the languages, this on the
book, is these meanings, and these
situations, that are made up, and in
fiction, as false, and as true, to the
individual reader.

The author from just one person's
discretion is warning, persons of interest.
He has intellectually made his writings,
to become of warning readers, from a
worded database, wherein, falsified
words, and fictitious meanings, are what
can differ, in circumstances. These
severe warnings, leads itself, to doing
wording, wherein the reader, is to be
recommended to be safe, at the
discretion of the author, from demoted
meanings, and these values, and their
safe, whenever reading books from the
writer, the reader's viewing
discretionarily, advised. Some adult
supervisions, in young ages of children,

way on up to what is of adult content, and adult consenting of ideas, are by the recommended, author of this book. By, reading these words of the knowledge of the author, wins in comparison of the works and the words, and the contrasting of the ideas and places, the world within, the words of genuine purpose, I think the reader will be warned, of the writing, if over too much bearing, in the life, of the situation.

Be cautious, in when reading this book, when adult's situation, from age is, a recommendation, because strength of words is a common, affect as overvalued. The expression of the words, and the wordings, of the writer's decidedness, is a warning to beware of in danger, of the thoughts and ideas. If an idea, as when expressed by a very American person, comes true, then words become meaningless.

The writer of this book recommends reading the messages from this book, as if the book was written books, to the book's messages of war, in true or false terms, of one opposite nations. The themes and the parts, of the well informed topics of third world wars, are

from the expressions, in what are of
reading lives from a viewer, as if this
viewer discretion, came from myself, as
in if, what suppositions, is in
recommended, by the writer.

Permissions of the Contacting In Words
of the Author –

Literal permission is to be asked, from
the reader of this book, to the author of
the book, as an, written letter, or email,
or sent piece of lettering, of the reader's,
of can be asked, of the reader, to contact
the author.
If, the writer, is asked from the readers
and fans, by you the readers of the book,
if it is allowed, to contact the author, you
may do so. Sometimes, the author in
gratitude of approved voiced messages,
and letters sent to his desk, then as of
letters and emails, are the exchanged
documents, then only used for – safety!
To the author, to contemplate, read, and
return, to the reader, all documents,
these are approved.

Warning A Book – American War

If, only one, of a reader should contact the author of this book, then thus, the both parties, should approve of implicate and meaning of the book, on only the writer's terms. That is in the situation, if this is not of a book positive message, from the approval, of general consented, books, as a matter to be discussed.

This is allowed, to the reader, by the author. Thank you, for the context, that there is a world of meaning, and in a wording, paraphrase, or sentenced offending or offensive, approach to the author, from the reader, then the author, is not responsible.

warning, and as an approved idealism, the context from expressed in general terms from the idea warning, what is about in the words in the book, are approved, as to be safe. However, in authoring the book, the author states subliminal messages, that are safe, and are not to be harmful, in what can become, very harmful, based on olden times. The writer, of this book, recommends a good frame of mind, in reading.

(The News In Times About Winning the
War From The American World Of The
"USA", In The "World War Three!")

The All-American Third World War's
Book!

The book I made, as a declaration of
war. I won, as a signed approval form,
of what I have done in life, and in how I
am from America, as the willing and
able, side. I, decided that as a newly
made nation of Americans, to side with
world leaders, to create oneness. I've,
decided minded choices, and actions as
by made up mindedness, of the one-
sided soldiers, of war. Them and
ourselves, from the presiding circle of
decision, wherein the every side, is of all
of only one part, is the one-sided shaped
full circles shape, that wins; wars! The
new forms as the shapes unfolding only,
are matched with penned signatures, in
world war three, of America's fates, is
decided on, by me. I, am only by

American terms, as the world leaders of
world war three, will decide on
declaration from the Christian, – "Three
World Wars!"

I am, the supported election, of war.
Presidential selection of follower, from
warring ideas, I am safe with, as
Americans. Yet, intelligent wartimes are
designed by intelligent, by its world-
war-Three's – Antichrist American's,
war's proven minds.
.
The World Leaders Symbolic of One
Music Man – Whom Plays to War's
Opened Wins!
The President Symbolizing American
Freedom From Choices, In The Music
Of The Leadership Of Wars, Is Played,
As "Hail To The Chief!"

- The Musical Man's Choir Conductor
From the Musical Man's War Chorus!

They are the symphonic chorus leaders,
behind the beautifully written musical
song playing, and vocal singing abilities,
in the notes of happy and sad,
movements and rises, that songs can be,
as much as played. A musical man,
conducts the chorus, of the symphonic

sheets of musical instruments, both human and musical, to lead the music world, with participants of the musical world's, musical sadness.

The President of the USA; Is a Happy Man!

The happy, man leads, all of this chorus, as his song, is beautiful in – "As Love!" "As Love", is the message deemed, not as in war, but as in peace, of all over the world.

To all, the voices that have heard the sounds of musical notes, as all being played in musical notes and the musical letters, that formed, in the music sheet's, hidden songs. The choral man, or instructed musician leader of the chorus headed by the conductor, lines of music came from the leading from the roles, of the music stand, and as the conductor, leads the singers, of the orchestra in how he, waves his baton in motions, the music is playing from the melodies, of sung and performed, songs of chorus.

All of the marching bands, from the voices of unison in song, lined up for the choral deformation from choirs singing songs. Over the loudness, sings the chorus from the voices, of high pitched musical notes, symbolic of the powers, for war. Times from need, resound from singing beautifully written songs.

I, have musical, instruments. To be played, in battle of written musical songs, from all formatted lines, directed by the orchestrated "baron", as the chorus leader, plays the musical instructions, of the songs. A.k.a., or in other words, the USA's Presidents in world wars, form alliances from the winning allied sided forces, all over the surface of the worlds takeover plans to find, out! In strategies, we allow the marching of men in formats of lines to go straight in lines, marching in unison, as the wars, for humanity in lives, get much bigger.

Nostradamus, a Doomsday Prophet, predicted World War Three. He, signed a symbol, of purpose in the geometry, in the building of a modern day new world order, from war's construction. He, is one of the Illuminati, of five most powerful men. He, is a fate, decider, if one nation of America, is to go, into war.

He, signs, the war documents, in the
American war's plans.

The sounds of the marching bands,
direct the formations to form lines in
wars, as we are taken out as the
country's, song followers of the beaten
path. In USA music, the mistrust of new
placed men of combat as leaders of the
free world, won by covering sides by
lands, in the air, and at sea.

The lines from the lives, of all of the
insides of the minds, and into the
intellectual aspect from man, come out
of the winning sides, the willing ways, in
the desire, of the wars!

We, must be one of the American
futuristic world wars, as formed from,
dealing with sides, to the USA deeds, on
the side, of warned warring wins!
Anybody, in the states, from war's
winning has costs of the victory, from
the help of the costs of the man, of must-
be situations, of humanly desire, from
winning the wartimes.

War won of the life in the American
circle, of winning wartime's – "USA
Presidents." In the USA word, action,

and response, helps to happen in the
standard designs of God, from the
ability, from the war's office, to help
riches, for people out! Those
businessmen, and the industry's men, try
to outdo, the output, of other countries.
The America, has the public knowledge
however small, it is going, to be. It is as
the willing citizenship, and from the
acceptable men from business. The
votes polls, are open today.

To reformed laws, of the nature of man,
laws are of the intellect. Wartime's
intellects, are from goals of, actions.
The instructed living places, are together
and in the oneness, of willing sides, into
war's life!

Therein lives in itself, within the
indwelled particles of these instruments,
to the formed lines, of the marching
bands, from what in intelligence is
formed from whose sides we are on, and
in what is formed as the past war, is
won!

To conquering all the lands, and
alliances of the countries, fighting as
sided by sided, marching feet, of the
war's shored island, across the view of

the mainland. In, an island lost at sea,
the actions from the war's leaders,
demise the desires to the formations of
soldiers, in unison in forms of marching
lines. All in this way on islands, go out
into the world, around us, in the trials
and tribulations, of lives everything
killing, into a factuality, of judges. High
at the seas, on an Atlantic Ocean Island,
stands all faced, warring scenarios of
demise, that conquer by winning. The
wars onto the deaths of invisibly warring
men, at war and in ways of killing, move
to the upwards inevitable sides, in all
wins of the third world war! Is, it
heroism, or acts of, warring sides of
American victories from, pigs in the
slop, or of the great American, warring
men?!!

Wins in the happiness of the thoughts of
the thinking, around the resounding
musicality to winnings from American,
and Allied Forces sides, wars are won
from the instruments played and, heard.
Musical instruments, as if the musicality
is played, are sounded off! The war's
march consists of men, marching two by
two, onto the battlefield of warring sides,
from every nation, every tribe, and
tongue and culture. The war's wins

totaled, are from the losses, of previous, world war two, battles of the all-around warring sides, from every single fight!

The desire of beautifully written words, in the notes, from the instruments of music play of horns, brass, and the bass and the treble, play notes from the musically sounded aloud, instruments. The sound, of the flute, is like the Angels singing war songs, for the winning of the wars! We, as musical masters, won! As if, the choruses with the leaders resound as like we are in wars, we unsound the resounding, from the lion's roar, in hell-bound actions, to act alone, on the staged, <u>war actions of life!</u>

They are the, musical leaders of the Americans, as their people, as human beings, as Christians, of all over, the USA. The people, of our forefather's lands, and our laws! The musical melodies, of the continue, as to play!! The harps, and the drums, of King David, are no match, for insanity!

The contrasts of the President, and the method of ironically playing of the notes of my music, is to the highest powers,

over the music! The American man,
God, and His "strings and the chords," is
– "The One World Order!" To, wins in
what we, have played from myself! Of
the world staged; music and song leader!
The – "New World Order!!!!"

The battle music, of "World War Three",
made notes sound, so beautifying and
resoundingly, chorus and the songs
from, the base to the drums, to watch the
wars in; "America"!

To Live And To Then Die Out Loud
Words From – "US and World
Leaders!!!" The war's musical times,
are arriving, in War's untied ropes,
around, "The American President," for
the excellence, on USA!!

To always make wars happen to the
winners of American nationalism, and
hiding plans, in stemmed wars in the
wartime game's wins, inside of the mind
attributes from knowledge, we decide as
the wins. But, wins over the Devil, how
do we, as Americans bring home, the
wins over the Devil forces, in warring
and fighting, on enemy's sides?!
Always, to be in the – USA! The USA,
is the golden fiddle, of Johnny, in

everywhere he plays, it, to beat the
Devil!!? Even in America, if in the
looks, of the State Flag, in the "Six Flags
Over Texas," won sides, then the Texas
Flag – Wins!

Empowering and overpowering their
forced positions of the world, in, "Three
World Wars," therein, is the fiddler.
Fiddles played the "golden songs," three
times, and in the Devil's name, the boy
wins! The golden warning sides, on
faced outwards, wins as its hands and
body, cover in death and, for extinguish
life. He, fiddled the win!

Playing the songs of the music man's
notes, won an all-American newspaper,
to write of "Johnny!" Any man, is a
fiddle player, too! The moral, to the
story, is that, all are equal, and are ready
and willing, to play a fiddle! The
"musician," adjourns the Devil's, fire
red courts, from Texas lawyers, in the
Wynne family of mine. The Texan
"smiling faces", and the willingly
wonderful leadership, is even as musical
roles, to every time, defeat the Devil.
The long music notes, of the golden
fiddle, is from how Johnny played, to the
Devil, to win all things, and in all defeat,

the Devil. I, am the fiddle player,
Johnny, and I play my fiddle, too. And,
when the Devil, was looking for a soul
to steal, I played the American
Presidential fiddle, and I won, the
"Golden Age," bid of music. I, played
my tune, to the Devil, to defeat him.
Then, to join the "New World Order." I,
duly and dutifully, all over the world,
from the level, age, and office, of the
Devil; outplayed the Devil. Then, I can
be – "The USA President!!!"

Philosophy from war, into what are the
positions of plotting powerful leaders,
whom lost in their characters, what is in
the golden age? To New World Order
and to winning armies, what is a winning
war?! Lead roles, that are therein
denoted as the sold and bought, golden
past from wars, from the golden aged, –
"new world order," has philosophical
contentment, in saving divinity's lives,
from the grace of God. The God of the
world, for worldwide wars, arrived in
Texas. The timing makers, of the
ancient past wartimes, on signaled, times
which were won, in these days, of the
wars, from one man's war dealt wars
with the, body of the – "The Tradition
Of The American President!"

To manage life, is to do the daunting
task of what war, is planned or
attempted, within the ideal and copied
methodologies, intellectually learned, as
in the technique from losses. We
succeeded in the new world order, in the
laws of war, of then buying the plans
into this persuading of them, or from the
American publics, to change their
decision on peace, and go onto – Three
World Wars!

War's frontal face I have seen, from how
of what it looks as an appearance, is in
its looks, of the worldly wars, of the
fighting from American wars, forming
an appearance, from what is, appealed to
the ugly! Marks on the foreheads of
children, from the antichrist, who lost as
tales are told, and as what are from the
stories told, and all of the heroic deeds,
warring ways.

"I am mad. Me, only of madness!
Three wars that won, of itself! The
complete wars is in all wars, Land is in
the envisioned allied forces, from past
olden, "the second world war", to
friendly forces, sided with America. The
allied forces, that won over, all of the

world war's, world stage, desired to be
on planet Earth!" The lands, that are
free and born American, and the alliance
of other country's forces, are the sole
reasons, that we are, living in the, "world
war's action!" Things forming of
whatever, is in another, world!

Powering, to the lost lives, of the
thoughtful life, from down at the
homestead, lives the Wynne family, at
the tradition of the family house, in the
living town, of Wills Point, Texas!
Within the Wynne's family tree, the line
of people, descend from southern grace
at the homestead in Wills Point, in, East
Texas!!!

In the Texas bloodlines, we all had
birthrights, in anyone of East Texas, as
chosen birthed rites! Life's chosen man,
is a family member, of the historical
Wynne family, Texan dynasty, of the
"Yet Another Glory," storybook wrote
by, "Margaret Wynne Harrison." The
songs of her writing, were almost as
gloriously illuminated shapes, as the Sun
in the daytime, and as the moon at
nighttime, and as the light of the Stars,
as the birthed Texas rites, as the Heaven
and Earth of the stars, that shine. To the

hands of time, and as relatives to the dynasty, of the Wynne family, I have won, over myself, in ways of war. War times, comes from all, its liberties, and willingness of the willpowers' laws. Lands of strong-willed laws, inherits in what is in all, I have learned, to be a true Texan!

I, have historically remembered the clan, and all of relatives from the "State of Texas," in the southernmost state of America's states or, nation-states, in the status, of my family, in the State of Texas. In family's lines, of the lands in over, the win's wars, as live the lowest shores of the Texas national state and freedom's shores. The lands, of trusted and truest American laws, live an ancient American Republic, of what or in, the state of what formed, a freedom and liberty, Republic of Texas, as it is called; home and freed land, land of – "Time!!!" New World Order based laws, cover the democracy. The State of Texas, succeeded, from the USA, to newest founded life, as only what the laws of the state, the rights, and the country's, succession from the land. The open lands from freeing the laws, and sounding the arms, of the truest

individual Texan liberties, and freedom
of the living rites, became their rights,
when Texas, succeeded. To the shores,
in its alone succession of America, the
Republic of Texas landed, on the
bottomlands, of the American shore,
bordering Mexico, as its American –
"Texan State."

The wars, from deaths, are alive. The
news from the stories of olden times, is
made possible, by world war three's,
supporters of the world war of
America's third time.
The antichrist wins, this war! In life,
antichristian Americans die, as the dead,
ends its life! Wars, of the life roots
being from the nature of man in the
antichrist, and the past history of its
lands, therein are living tree roots of the
family, as traditional wonders, of the
olden days, invoiced in checks, and the
expenses from family's finances loaned
out, from fun with family love, and
natural Texans. All-time knowing what
is fun, for us and, only we alike, in
family! Whatever, in what wars, bring if
not wars, lost; but won over lives, are to
the costs therein, invoiced in the checks,
from the Wynne family, going bankrupt,
from bills. What is now a Texan, is

what from known about historical roots,
therein is, a big Texan member's family
line, of relatives from birthright,
marriage vows, and lifelong wills, and,
rituals from, family line. The shadowed
tree, lies hidden family deaths, in the
past wars.

From famous Texans, on arrival of
parties, in how America talked of above
and beyond, well over, one hundred and
fifty, years ago! Wynne family, of five
hundred related Texans times from aged
lives, in the living clans, of the Texan,
Wynne family lifestyles, and traditions
of the Dallas, Texas, crowd of, family
members, from Texas, in the American
"USA". Family's stories, born long ago,
always seek out, the same mark, on the
humanity's frontal faces, to see the
standards at fun and sought out lives,
Wills Point, in Texas! Fates from
ourselves from whenever we fight a war,
life came around, giving not at alliances
but, intellectual discourse, brought forth
in its, sold general settlements.

The story of every tale, of the, "USA
War!!!!" For the Antichrist's American,
positions of power and involved roles of

leadership in acts from brave ambition,
converting the freedoms, of the warring
sided versions, of the American souls,
involved inside of the office of the
President. In intelligence, we are the
historical channeled winning sides, of
the US movement, of – "Antichristian
America!" War history's third, world
war, is from where I got my vision from,
in Chicago, is in what as, to endue me
into an oath of office in war, that was to
lead all of America, in "World War
Three!!!"

This is as one man, and as in being one
US President, in fighting of the third
world war, as its solely accomplished,
envisioned man from wars!

In the designed agendas, of the
consignment of the pastimes' war
deaths, in what this is happening in
world war, happen as the design and
equality, on the laws, for justice and of
the "USA President!" Writings, on war
books, made all of the USA, to warring
intelligence to win! Allow people, to
eradicate the forces, of darkness.

In history from living life, if three wars,
is made by me, and then I make the

deaths inside and out, very happening. I
am a natural born, Texas citizen. I, grew
up, the same, as any other, American.
Yet, my life is not yet, that of a soldier.
I, have opened up, the door, to war! I,
opened the pen, with bold letters, and
red ink, to signatures of all of the
American Founding Fathers, or US
Presidents, sealed by God.

I, will write cursive letters, of my pen in
hand, I wrote wars. Won in my own
writing source, we held all of, writings
sacred. In the ending of times, life as the
personalized life, follows any one, from
any thing, waged on the wars what is
then waged, on American, liberty.
Someone from American lives, is the
truest kind of one national victorious
man, made liberating laws and
lawfulness, from legendary and pastime,
lands of freeing; soils. Hand and boned
skin, not all tried and, tried and truest,
are wars, that are only wars. To this
ends of days, and in history from wars of
won, times one and only, complete the
cycle of war! I written in words, that
follow from actions, made war.

I've habitually formed, new habits of the
made wars, in the times of new world

order's, social and political, office, from
the war desk, seeing things, actually
from my ownerships, of the wooden
desk. I, won in my hands, the sword.
The pen over the sword's stone, taken
out, of the world wars, that are as the
victory, in every hand won.

These pens, and sword, as drawn oaths
and offices, from spending times, in my
lifetimes, came out of what are from
collaboration, in the new world order of
the age, end of penmanship or penned
writings, and ended winning of wars.
Swords, and truths, pen and stone,
unleashed from world war's nuclear age,
of war. Riley Miller, will to have wars
declared, war in the faced following,
onto the worlds, of the world leader.
The mindful, and intelligent, brains of
the soldier, have found a new leader of
American freedom, and justice.

To the endings of the world, we have
won this surmising task, in itself as a
daunting task of surmising knowledge
from difficulty, proven one day, onto
this day in time, to have won, all world
wars. To sell souls from military
soldiers, are to following parts, of wars
and in this lifetime's peace, obey these

instructions of war, in the new world order, of every common American. Do not discover evil souls, in the evil's; of ways, to the good of Senators, of the USA!

The three-sided arguments of life, are as applicable, as what are, in a period of, 1. The USA Intelligence, 2. In World War Three, 3. The American President, 4 The Presidential Staff and 5. The Bible Antichrist, 6. The USA End Times; to wins, all from its, over everything. Lifetimes, I have tried wherein the USA public disagreed and publicized television, on the war ring's sides, and war's viewers, of me, that can become an available publication, on the, Wartime's Manual On WW3.

Inside of the book, is writings in the instructions, onto wars, and battles being fought! Wars, onto the American manual writings, on the desk, of mine at my parent's, house. Its, what is, ever the made-in and Washington D.C. man's, what is for the sole use, and sole distribution, for this American wars designed system, of the American, "World War Three." I, am the man, whom to all, is writing into these books,

that are in made to succeed life, and that
are inside the art of living, that is in the
America's dreamt, living ways that wins,
all-time's over the intelligence, of –
"WW3!"

America, in the endings from everyone's
life, and in the beginnings of everyone's
deaths, we complete, days of our
country, from wars to create, three wars
– overall in its –"World War Three." I,
am in the American President's
Warring' Office!"

This is the battle plan, for this "New
World Order." I am on the side that
wins. The battles and wins, to the point,
from the Americans, would be whatever,
from whomever, wins my war, or my –
War Office!" For everyone, to "Follow
The Yellow Brick Road!"

I am, Riley Miller! And I am, war's
writer. In, this book of my work, I
sincerely worked times and times, again,
to simplify my philosophy from wars.
It, is that war is good in the USA, for
something, named all of us, as
America's, followers of a Massive
World War – The War Of Jesus Christ,
World War Three!

America as in Antichrist of war, is timed
as overtimes, in terms of a "third world
war". To be in the shores of an
American – wins!

Warring philosophy, of man whose
words I am in the endings for warring
times of my life. I won, over sentenced
deaths, of soldiers, by myself in office,
future from all, from the waging of
"World of War III"", at work.

I, am in the beginnings, won are that
from slavery, and of freedom's notorious
voiced USA servants, made of the
promised land of remade winning, from
sold warring surmising, proclaimed
peaces.

We as Americans, won of the
beginnings, and in the office of
wartimes, a world ally and a new
worldwide humanity, will end, all of the
days, of this war!

The annihilation of humanity, from what
is called the American third democracy's
war! The American Americanism
automatic aged weapons, are from wars,
are over deeds, of humanity's sold,

battle-born, and American armed,
countryside, worldwide killing
machines. towards entirety of the
armies sizes, seize an American battled
state, or Warring Superpower!

The proliferation, of one man, "World
War!"
The war is on, and in this book, of
declarations. The war's independent and
fighting book's sold message is to recruit
all Americans to world war, of
America's three, or, the American third
time. Instructions in war, of literature
and powers! This is on the manual, onto
these powers, of the insane book, in
intelligence. Now soldiers, are for war,
become recruited, programmed minded
wars, from the fighting worlds, of
America. The third America, won over
every American ism's started fighting,
from the wars, and soldiers, from the
fighting, of the ancient times, of the
America independence, to win again, in
our nation's, "New World Order's Age!"

Only America, wins three wars. A new
ordered oneness, of a new professed
birth and admittance, came in the United
States of America, President's office.
The President Barack Hussein Obama, is

the name, from the America's, leader. In
ages of war, and in moldings the form
from freedom, the lands of America,
participants from the model age, is
another third, world war's age. To
winning wars overnight, the careful
planning of powerful sources, firstly
knows America, and secondly; recruits
worldwide USA, wartime's winning,
dominating sides. The third aged,
warring America, is of the American –
"Third World War!?" The fighting of
soldiers, the recruiting of soldiers
fighting, then the soldiers of America
killing, the US is fortuned, for peace!

"The USA!!!" The President of the
United States of America, is the leader
of the "free-world!"
The War Office, in is warring ordered
plans of war, sides within the homeland,
the other worlds, and the third age of the
man – in New Order of the World.

I willed, to formed proclamations of
justice, and decrees for freedoms, in
wins over all, of every land, culture, and
nationality.

Land firstly established as, "America's
War!" The highest position of power, in

the nation of, "America," is the President of the USA! Inside of war, in the intelligent life, of the foreign lands, and tested famed countries, and not lands on this surmising positioned countries, the best from the lands, is the free-world, of the USA, in figures of powerful people, and leaders, and positions of Presidents from other nations, we can, "Win WWIII!"

From our times, and the circumstances, from everyday livings, and unto another everyday dying, units of uniting, all of America, as leader of the third world war. Laws, measure and, spoken in word and in writing, a deed beyond, themed storied, world-war three, of the soldiers! Always, in deeds and works, the President of the United States, is elected in the public office, for popular vote! For the most impressive book, on war of themed office, concluded three worldwide wars ago, and announcing to bring – "World War Three!"

In the Office of the Chief of Staff, or the Presidential duty, attention to the plus and minus, of war, is of sides! Americans, always picked as only Americans, die to live, the greater life,

that I hope concatenates the manual for
war, in the hands of good personalities
can defeat the evilest personality of,
arguments of wars.

The third war, is mine before the
Doomsday war, begins and ends, in
"Nuclear War!" Americans, warring the
battles, and choosing the world war,
shall see a winning world, over what is
evil, bind and ensnare, nationalism and
democracy, over laws of our country!
The Oval Office, the White House in
D.C., and the Senate, House of
Representatives, and the Staff of the
American Presidency, is all summed up,
to wars, even American, sided wins,
defeating deaths the USA, way from life.

Strong willed, reading books, the High
Seat of American roundtable, the hand
and chair, is willing for the Christian
leader, in choices to sit in the seat, in
highest precedence of the one man's
nation. The followers in parties, from
American's national states, the USA, by
one choice of one voice in actionable
chairs, from Senators, supported side of
laws, by matters of deskwork, in
conjunction of passing of the bills, in
wooden support, the President's chair,

pen, in hand, and the desk, opens, and
closes, the door, the hand opens!

Welcome home, Riley Miller, we should
enjoin to the fourth of July, of American
beauty of lands, flags, and stripes, of red,
white, and blue. To, on the risen pride,
for the American flag's, victory over
all's World War Three, of the American
minds. The mind of victory, is from the
American flags. These, are freely
flying!

To be in these times, is sad. I, want to
know more, about World War Three, in
flags! These are the surrounding, and
the difficult times, of a great depression?
The polls are closed down!?

Duty, Service, And Honor of the Third
World War Times – Dedicated In Is
Fullest Life, Into The Biggest Star, In
the American Homeland.

A Free-World – From Texas, To
Entering Nations!

To Enter Into The Winning Sides of
Freedom of State of Texas Republic,
Texas Tradition, Texas Great and Big
and Lone Star State's, Honored Soldiers,

The Tried and Truest Birthplace of
Mister Riley Miller –

The Texas Birthed Stars, In The Wynne
Family of Texas!
The Fame of Members, Miller Family,
of Riley Miller's Fortune's Roles of All
Trusted, And Official Families!

To – The Great State of Texas!
To – The "United States of America"

To – The United States of America's
Presidential Roles, and the
Representatives of the Oval Office From
the USA Presidential Position, and the
USA majority elected voting count, the
President race for Office, from the
Minority vote, the USA's Staff from
workers in the White House, the USA
Senate and its Represented Members of
the US Senator Floor, the House of
Representatives, and to Congress!

Inside of the mind, of my Wynne family!

The United States Presidential Oval
Office, and to the USA Senate, of the
House of Representatives, as my native
Texan, lead role as life, wins as the

Great State of Texas – "Wins WWIII!"
From my minor role of writings, for
wartimes' President, and above anyone
elected, I have won it's all, and I've
won, everyone in all three times, of the
American war's, titled books!!!

I ask no to, other writer, as theirs in
wars, of these comparing myself, to
Prince William (Wales), from the people
from who know my books! To the
Electoral College, of the Popular Votes,
for the – "USA Presidential Title!"

I, have won, the world's over all the
forces, in this life, and so on, in the –
"Life As Wins!" Or, the Wynne's
family, from Dallas, in the Great State
Of Texas!!

Alliance, of an impossible job, does to
makeup, an official leader's role, in the
third world war, of world war three's,
persona, in the Trinity's, from Texas! A
war story willingly told, of persons, in
office representatives, World War of a
third time, in Doomsday, Texan, in
starry eyes! I wrote over ninety books,
as in, written in an imagination book's
world, of the United States people, of the
American states. I cannot attest, ever

being, for myself, I live in living, as
Christ. As, good as gold, can I sit, and
write in the best-ever, ninety books, of
the mind's end, as happens the power at
the end's promoter; as another literature
writer's life, from a lifelong role of
mine, in what I wrote, how as, a
numbered list, of – "91 intelligent
books!"

USA's Presidential life, in all the life's
Bibles, as from an aged Kingdom
secretly, indelibly planned, and hand
written, as the books, on the dull life, of
mine – "For An American President's
Desk And War Office."

As By The Author – Riley Miller, As
The Writer!!
(For The Reader)

As American, Right and True, Natural
Texan – As An Christian And American
New World Order's; Own and Loaned;
"USA Presidency" – The Life From
World of, "World War Three"!

Wartimes –

My Living Strong-Willed Persons, All
Win War's Together, In Their Life's

Games, Found Out Everyone In Our
Lives' Business Deals; From Therein
Politics Of Circles, At The Top's Wins
Above Christ, Won On Popularity
Votes!

All-Knowing God's Willing Texan State
Republican, Christian of Churched Of
The PCUSA, I Love Game of War's
Books!!!" With Wins – In The NWO!

My Goal to Win – "The New York
Times", Best-Seller's List!!! The –
WWIII of the Dallas Morning News!

"My War's Willing Then Totaled Life"
By – President Riley Miller

One Quote As In
For World War Three –
(The Second Adam)

The rebirth, of Adam, as my
depicted soul!!! The advent of
world war three, is the fall of
man, and the reinvention of, the
human man. His desire, seems to
be, to have the fallen
knowledge, of man. Adam, fell
in the beginning, then this will
also, happen once again. "

Chapter 1

All War Is Inevitable –

As of now, in America, there are
winners and losers. The entire country,
is of leaders who, run the world from
itself, sited is in these times of need. In
the Holocaust, of WW2, came Hitler.

From Russia, the "Cold War!" And the
US, terrorists??? I, will not ever, forget
– "9-11!" The entire world, watches.
America is its friend. But, what happens
in Antichrist life when, all nations are
from – "War Evil?"

Will, all Americans, still live, their life,
to the fullest? I, do not know, ask
"Young Life!" Ask, "Joe White!" Ask,
"Jesus Christ; Our Lord!"

In, the year of 2000, I saw Heaven. I
saw castles. It is in a vision.

In, 2009, I saw the – "Antichrist." He,
ruled with an iron fist, that is a – "666."
He marked everyone. He was the mark.
He, led us all, into World War Three! I,
was in, vision. Now, I have an,

"attitude." I think, I can lead, the American war.

However American wars win, and from the costs of war, Germany loses, the last battle. The Americans, in the costs, of the fairy tales, of stories, in the everyday life of mine, came from data. The data, from the computer, keeps records, of USA knowledge. The Illuminati, we all see, just watches, all of, the – "USA!" In world war three, I am the victor.

One day, I've seen all this data. All I did is, "look". Then, what appears in USA data now is, however the, "New World Order," became mine, of the Illuminati, from America. I, now will, fight for you, and I will win! The America I knew is willingly mine! I, shall win, everyone over. One day, I want to win. All of the world, I will, this want, into winning. This is to belong, to my, world will. I will join, the Internet's Illuminati.

From this data, the illuminati, controls the world. The entire world version, of World War, is of World War Three. History's story is the America's, "black magic". This enemy, I must remember. It, Wars, itself.

The USA's Illuminati, and in losses, I,
do not know how, that World War
Three, will ever, end up as American.

I do! I know how! This is it! The world
war three; it will begin now. Show this
battle, which is an everyday battle,
which it is, up to us, as. To stop, the
American tradition, from losing, ends
this confliction, of the American flag.

We all, in victories, must win. This war
time, just has to be, over wins. This
country stands the test of time.
Eventually, our USA will win, over all.

This stands up, and into alive in the new
aged, "USA People!" All, I know in this
new world order's time, is that we will
win in, the world war of – "WW3"!

Supporters, from the streets, of Babylon!
All nations, win the test of times!
America is, to solve all. Heaven, and
Hell, knows. The world, and that of
which tells, the story's entire plot!
America, wins! If, of World War Three,
then all will, win!!! I promised, all of
you, only to this, factor – "to win!"

Words Of Wisdom

"To cause having life, to be from what
America decides, there must be a war,
and in its place, arrived in this place, the
sides of good and evil, to overcome the
injustices. Only, one winner!"

– As An American Fallen Soldier, I Fall
Off The Planet's Edge – In to the, "New
World Order!" The Return, To Earth,
From Every Fallen Race.

- Riley Miller

From the American side, of this story is
about, only wars. In the "Nazi Germany
days", wars won. Histories, decide!
Germany, knew this is about, how the
American war, loses. That negatives, is
if, all madmen, control the world. This
is, from the new world order, and from
America's losses. This country, wins
with the New World Order. There, are
peaceful states, of the order. The world
order's callings, is to collect the collect
call. Presidents, own it. Delegates,
decide on it. And, America reacts
solely, to itself, in laws.

Losses of the life from our country, all
tell about the victory, from the lost lives
that are, in the daily, battles, and wars.
A war, of World War Three, is
inevitable, in the history, from
Americans. Only the good side wins.

The warring countries, in this time, are
China, Germany, and Russia. The wars,
at the endings of the days, are the
Antichristian, Anti-American wars.
They are counted, as God's Holy Bible,
of meanings, that we cannot fathom,
with wars.

They are the top dog's, biscuit, and
bones. They, as Americans, are the top
dog's, law abiding citizenship, and
respected councils, from whom, lose the
war. Never-ending stories, plagiarized,
the Holocaust, as what the World War
Two's, endings, condoned. This is, the
moral of the story, which as of one
Christian, in the world, I, have made
significant, progress, in this life, and, in
Heaven. Why Heaven, is only an idea?

In my life, I cannot fathom how life, on
the Earth, is history's lie. Even
Germany's, feared Adolf Hitler won,

WWII! An autocracy so big, that from
the Holocaust museum, the victims were
wiped clean. The entire beautifully
worked, tale of soldiers! An, entire
country, became blamed, of victimized
races. The Jewish, people were, so lost.

All, demands of his philosophy! All due
to fallen times, what is historic, is due to
the fallen knowledge, from the snake.
Why is it in life that won over Jesus
Christ and God and the Holy Spirit, why
evil wins? Why, is it to everyone, in this
war's pastimes, of death's life, and of
this, world war three ship, comes the
sinking sailors? The man of history's
life, that fame, power, and glory, cannot
forget – 'World War Three!"

Some say Communist people, are
victims, of World War Three???
Therein life peaces, is not eventually
traced back, to America, as one country!

There, are also China, Russia, and Japan.
The countries, of sin, are these countries.
The Nazi Communists lost of World
War Two. Their plan, from the
Communists, is to make the whole, "new
world order", only the enemy, as the
country, of theirs to lose. The book

looks good in ideologies, but the
enemy's contextual analysis, is eventual.

The found life, from the underground, of
America, eventually shows, its face, in
WW3!! The version of life, for the poor,
is starvation. The mad world, war
undoes in America. The innocent, of
counted lives, are hidden from countries.
These treasures in Heaven are only, from
an afterlife. Love of thy brother, lies
from the heart to hell, spoken in tongues,
hiding, what cancer is hidden in courts,
of justice. The nicest world, of everyday
life, is all gone. Just picture hands of
history, made in liberty; on this title of
war, from justice, in the US "Supreme
Courts!"

Whoever is evil is dead? Whatever is in
lying goes to jail, on Bibles? What costs
of life? Whose surrendered life is made
out of American history's freedom?
Who is controlled by a false desire?
Why, is to make God proud, in those
whom loved, an evil life? Why is the
best, of the best only, if surrendered?

Why is not, one man, always not to a
false religion? We are definitive to the
USA's fallen soldier, as to everyone.

If in worldly evil times, we win. In world war three, or Texas in true world wars! Why, is all those victims, came from, knowledge? Those whose image we reflect, as our fallen idols, realize war, as evil. Why is the fallen man of Adam, from the history of doubt?

Do, you really know me, or my evil in the thoughts? I know your living days, on then thinking lives, of your own, eventual thinking! I am not, why you are, the thinking man, of thoughts!

I have a good country. I have forgivingly, thanks Adolf Hitler, for World War Two. I must respectfully, wanted to bring this world, into the peace of the world. Go towards, the goal. Make my mark, and stand up, to be a, true hero of, "A Man America's tradition".

God came into the world. He desired to be, loved as every good American, are to be loved! So much happens in war, from that in one land, and in another lands, we still are fighting, clashing in sides, gone mad in wars. Freedom, is freeing, in the lands of war. History is

one big, lie. In this history, there are
world wars. In the life of mine, I
believed in God.

In war times, we are all alive. We have
democracy in life, and in this, living
democracy. The life, of mine is freedom
based. Intellect in power, control end
and beginning, as freedom based,
puppets. Puppets; are not the masters.
That is solely, it, in wars.

Puppets are ours. People, will win wars.
So will puppet masters, if they believe in
us. Why believe in power? After three
wars, we are exampled to win.
Americans, to the raw power, directs
why democracy, only wins, in world war
three.

Sands of new times are covered, over the
sands of ancient America, in the ancient
aged old times. We all, arrived on earth,
from an age old order, of the age of sold,
histories.

Now, after old times, we've recovered.
The new age ordered, of the man from
the war. We, at these times, are already,
at an age, of war. Following the ancient
Freemasons, is the 'new world order," of

man's, lost democracy. War, in the golden times, when democracy ruled the country, was in the Founding Father's story, of America.

Stories are told, from history's pages. To American's wins, which are from what history's wisdom affects, see in the eyes, of an old man. His worldly perspective, completes days, of wins from war? By the graces of one man and war, I thank, ancient times that were hard. All people have lived, in the ancient ages, on the display, at the history museums.

Forget, that in needy times, we are to be liked, in their religious persecutions. All, by the British Americans, on the war's terms. The absolute wartimes, count down to doomsday, when Armageddon, happens, to innocent people. Why in wars, are wins only? To be just in fight, that is in fought, to win? In this, is our America? The battles of Armageddon are not fought, to be won!!

The history is the best, at war! I still, have lived life, in its studied, nature! I sometimes, really cannot judge; of Jesus Christ, in whom, or is in God. The

American soil's land, is into the chosen
lands, as if we go, ask until I am going,
onto war in American grounds.

Lands and seas, as if, we are counted in
America's number, are in the wars, as is
of lost or won victories. Our history, on
open pages, is made of lands to winning
sides, and seas, to winning countries. All
will, win. We will win wars. The war's
property, on winning sides, is from
winning or losing sides, of the world
over.

The history that we are in, is then land
chosen. The playthings that we grow up
with are gone, unless we win, over
American's soul, in its entire all. The
choices, in all countries, are on,
whomever, are dependent on whom,
have the winning sides. We, all love
war. The land of the free, is not dead,
but alive.

Due to wars, we are lost, in living.
Three sides, to all winning, of three
wars, are our, mark. I, want to make, a
mark on man.

One person's, new world order!!! But,
his is, the principle of this all, therein is

into, the safety, of the country's life. If one country attacks, on America soul, as the fired shots, fights back, then in war's life, from these losing, situations, comes losses, from the President of the United States of America. But, if a President retaliates, he dies, themselves as countries die, and all hell willing, he breaks loose, over history's, all. The President, can be shot. This is the worst crime, in thinking's nature.

We always, must account, for all lost lives. The world's blamed, die off. The numbers, from times at hand, of individuals fighting in wars, came from wartimes, then come from history, as its pages unfold, from world wars. But, we are never the puppet-masters of democracy, or the puppets from abuse of justice. We are all soldiers. We, win wars.

In books, and inside writings, we exist as but just soldiers, of fortune. By, having lives, lost, soldiers lose, what are in lands needed, in times of war. The absolute winning side is America. I have sold this idea, to many people. The history is, from that which is being, on all the sides, of their justices, and is in

lost countries, and the lost democracies,
of America.

How we live, is in how we are to swim
to the shores, together. As one, of the
greatest American body of water, the
Biblical Jesus Christ, walked on. Win
its pride, and then I can make, these
men, to the shores of history's America.

To win, in just a price, to pay, there is no
cost of amounting, in deaths. Towards
the day, when we win, three world wars,
the hand of the ancient Serpent, or
"Dragon", is covered. The United States
of America's, best followers, are the
United States of America's followers,
and are in, the newly made loved life, of
this life's living. Living creeds, which is
to not ever help all people, is to help
you, to all my riches.

My life is centered on Young Life
camp's people. I row, in easy times.
But, we are in hard times. Wars, are in
this country. Deaths, in tomorrow's
times, are to belated, irony.

When wars happen, the war's camera
will film. The media, from the times of
world war three, is how we will

communicate. We, came alive past
doubts, arrive of the countries of war.

So is talk, of the New Jerusalem. I, find
out what this is, with Jesus Christ.

I am paddling harder. I am, knowingly,
am increasing. Then I see the shore. In
my boat, and with the more effort, I sail.
I set sail, in the boat. I, am gliding
across a lake. I arrive, to the shores. I,
with my friend, cross safely.

On the other side, is the Earth's
Heaven's, living, castles in the sky? I
lived, a vision, in Young Life camp, of
the "New Jerusalem." I saw my,
Heaven! And, I am happy. I am just a
man. I do not know how a man ever? I
sailed, in a boat? I've, have had my
visions.

My vision of my life, in this, is in what
is, true as my Father's – "Friend!" Hell
is within him. Shores on the other side,
he carries himself, in the boat, to dry
land. God wins, in my mind – "Jesus
Christ!"

The America he sees beautifully is
guaranteed his, as an ongoing life. His

life history, form in the scenario from
world war three, hates the worlds of
hate. Here is the example, acting when
this is, alive.

In and from, how I have fought, inside of
the intellect of God, in the world, from
wars. Schools, all over the world's
people, have neglected young minds,
and disregarded teachers. And the goal
wins in learning. Whatever is another
mission, of what I am in, is from how I,
came from, a new, another side, of war.
Americans lose. We, in all things, and
in olden times, are lost, in the media.
The losing of American values, in
whatever, is in war's mind, of Christ!

All deaths, win, in what is meaningless.
Life, is not, everyone's good. Choices
and opportunities in America are for
men, in the school systems, which get us
started in wars. I, see wars, with some
of the greatest people, seeking me out, as
the winner of World War Three. Was
not that what, I was promised, in this
good life? What history, does not know,
is that war Generals, and are crazy.

As, life of, in a boat captain, and asks,
what might I asked not of his, then, he

took his knife, and then took his life.
Sin, knifed everything, of winning
therein are not, worth living in, the one
and the not another situation, by the
America soil. I, have failed. I cannot
mean, to lose, in a life's – war situation.
In my life, by and by, I lose an egg.
That egg is the life of me. That egg is
scrambled.

In, whatever I am gliding into as in, one
man. From whomever, he is faster in
war. Lands are his, then made faster. If,
I loved, in an American way, is it the
ending forever, for my life? War, is in
these opened seashores, and skylines of
our country. I am paddling toward, the
ocean's edge, and Satan's war of Hell.
My hatred lives inside, too much
thinking. I, live in the traded life. One
and only, America only lost.

If only, I lived alone, then I would, in the
American tradition, dream the American
dream, and make American my home. I,
love successful, people. What make
sense, in the homes of mine, am me. I
am an American homeward bound, to
live in this country. In the past, nothing
mattered. "I love America."

I've, lost myself once. In knowledge,
who dared from dream? Perhaps,
toward the dream, living consequences,
is the third world war. His love is to
love a girl. If I, loved her. She is my,
Miss America, involving support, to her.
I will hold her dear.

I was my old girlfriend's friend, and a
lover. But, she was mentally, as an
illness, was known to happen to her,
"mind". She was an outpatient example
at, an American mental hospital, known
as – "Hope!" As, she fights to stay
alive, I must not protect and know her,
she calls herself, but she is mentally ill,
at what matters in world war three.
Mass, I do not know her.

In the American tradition, of forgiving.
Above the skyline, I've, seen all kinds of
people, in all ways, of life. This is my
father's land. I now cannot see dead
people. In this life, and in my last dying
death, I cannot, die.

This is because I have Jesus.

Life, as is promised, not to kill you. The
meaning of man is in the American. He,
knows your life, and your death's plans.

Hell he wins, how he can fight a victory
war, over you, and not, your happy lives.
His, is United States of war, calling.
Understanding is in war. He calls his
father.

His nation is at home. He wins, and eats
dinner, at the same, kind of meal, with
the same, kind of people, as them. He,
cares a lot, for the American tradition,
peace is so much harder to maintain
when you are high. The lands of
America, from mine, are what is the
chosen lands of the promise of the war,
in the land of the free.

The home, of the American brave
peoples, that I knew is free, is home. I
like, to call America, home to, everyone.
Wars are easy. If I start people, in world
war three's ideology, all then, for a
people win, a historic feat.

And as the forest's trees, hide. And,
attitudes, on the boat glides, and as the
reflection of the crystal castles, are what
I stare at, and see, with a view, of
Saranac Lake, New York.

My plan is to divide the American
waters, with bad irony. I, have loved
Jesus Christ, but I, always also loved,
God much more! I have sailed the seven
seas, wherein everybody is looking for
something!

But as comes, what of nothing, but war,
in my big life. I envision World War
Two, like this, vision. In order to cross
the shores and make it to the other side, I
go across, wherein I go, and will go,
swimming.

Nazi, Germany's Hitler's, becoming
famous, came of war games. All wars
were not war games at all, but examples
of hate. Expenses in this free life, paid
of queens living at the top, are not, worth
this cost.

If I win, the war games from the top
dreams, Jesus Christ, is in this life, as
counted, then that is at all new world
order. In, these expenses, pens are
futile. The chosen lands, in the Holy
Bible, were written of, by Moses!! He
must win. He, saved the chosen, by
parting the Red Sea. Water, is able to
drown you, in the same way, that slavery
is what, attempts to know, my God's,

naturalistic nature. We are all, that which drown at sea, unless we are chosen, by the chosen by, History's God's people. What, if I am not? Life, in the land of the Promised Land that as not in Heaven, does anyone ever drown, but cannot is, by men, of honor as in who commit to – "Jesus Christ.

Some ever enter ingoing, that never again, from the shores of America, will I swim alone, perchance. In world war, I am swimming. As I may never go to sea, I will, not go alone. If I, ever again, go to world war three's, I will be prepared. My America is due to Jesus Christ. He is life, from the shores, in a foreign land.

If I can seek the American gold system, to see myself, crossing the lake, then I am a homebound person. To cross, the lake is my greatest desire, in life. If I, want to be myself, as I see the things, in war, all of myself, is then going back and forth, to the end world, of the new world order, of America's. Waters high, not going overboard, of the showing of the darkened waters, in the crystal life, of the story's past.

The colored rainbow, is in the sky,
where Heaven and Earth, combine sides,
is from what colorful. Colored, from
one shore of beauty, as hand and hand,
life wins by crossing the body of water,
to make it to the shore. Across the lake,
swims all of your life, with another,
able-bodied person. I swam, across the
water, to the Kingdom of Heaven.

God knows Himself. The loved war has
itself, a God. If He loved war, then the
entire world would be His. Life, fallen
the same. And, from Jesus Christ, in
little times, came along, in friendships,
to lead the masses, astray. This is
according to the American people.

American empires were lost, in the olden
days. To, those who lived a life, I thank,
every one of you. The person you are
measured by is seen in court, as "always
loved". For all, who loved you, as, my
Americans, and in life as mine, some
day, I will thank you, in the top-secret
spot. Does, anyone read the Holy Bible,
from God? Must I respect your choices?
In world war, we are sacrificed as lambs,
in this frame, of mind to the USA,
people.

Everyone, we all know about, talk about,
how life, and war enemies, can talk.
They speak, of world war's, plagiarism,
in lost times. How the American,
intellect and, smiling faces, of the lost
America, and its everyday losses. We,
lead over all, about the life, of the world
war three, from an American
perspective, of a natural war's leading,
person. I am an American President,
and as a person, I can see you. I can see
all of you, and, then in this knowledge,
and what is seeing what, in the world is
about the world war three.

I am alive, in whose country, that this is
about, is into the, "Mad World." From
the shores of the Young Life camps,
castles in the sky, I saw once, in the
vision of mine, where I learned to swim,
into the "World War Three," waters. I,
have been, told that I, was a great leader.
As one American, came to know as, an
American mindset, then is of itself, in
the knowledge of itself, who tries, this
hardest to win!

Wins over what is in all, of America.
Written philosophy, in books. The
triple-sixes as a man! The false animal,
in Revelations. The beast, dwells within

hearts! Then, it is in this life – threefold.
The Holy Bible, can be true. In words
the accepts history, nations approval.
Riley Miller, as a Texas, accepts
legalism! The first, and last, step to the
Antichrist, of American peoples.

Evil of mine. I knowing animal and
man, in duality, of both sides, winning
and losing, in world wars! War is in
what it takes from presumably, the
Antichrist, in who life, loses in works.
The works, that himself takes on, to win
the third world war, is asked, by only
three men.

The three kings, of the Antichrist, or
"tripled-six," man of numbers. On, my
forehead history's war, is a six, six, six,
mark! Threefold, on threescore of the
number, "666". Marking the number of
six-hundred and sixty-six, as three sixes,
adding up to six-hundred and sixty-six,
or three numbers, of the digit six, as one
marks from the forehead! The sixes, of
the numbered, triple-six digits of three
sixes – "The Man of War!" In the
Hebrew language, the mark identifies
him. The Bible, understands him. The
Antichrist, won. The Antichrist, and

Christ, lives in! The soul, is the
indwelling place, for their bodies.

Jesus Christ knows me. I, have been
saved, by Jesus Christ. Christ, is not the
Antichrist. The world, is for myself.
This is if, I believed in Christ in three
wars, of world war, three times. If, I can
live, inside of these, deaths. Then, I
would make amounts of banking,
money! But, what does, not come from
Jesus Christ?

In America, the Antichrist's America,
and what is about me in times, and what
concerns that is about the Bible, is of
God. I can know that the world war
happens, overnight with the Illuminati's,
army of darkness, and army of goodness.
And, from the American Dream, is the
Antichrist, coming of the new world
order, in the age that is from evil men,
compared to all, we all will win, with
Devil victories, but not in this lifetime's
dreams.

My life, then is good. I am elected
President, in what I am now forming of
America, and in the visions of the New
World Order, comes world war three. I
can see, in which comes truest, in the

America, of mine, wherein this war
happens. Overnight, war itself is going
to happen. My life is in going to World
War Three, all is going, to be mine.

In itself, and from my life, came the life,
and in I believed in, the American, of
"World War Three!" To demand in fact,
about what is about these wars, in this
book, that I win over all with, which is
in from the writing, that is of mine. The
real idea, behind of the American dream,
is in the "Antichrist!"

America's whom is then going to war, to
become crazy, as the American people.
To follow the leader, and see what wins,
we must follow the Antichrist of
America, to see life. Then the America
wins, in the third endings, of the third
times, of the third world war, of the third
person. The dream, of the American
Antichrist, of wars comes true, in the life
chosen, to the wars.

I, follow war's denials, of that event,
which is so very crazy, that the
situations, in how we react, are even
having world war three, which sees
wars, as the annihilation of the human
race. The purpose from this war, in the

life of mine, is to become the winner, as a winning part of America, as the war itself, moves on larger attitudes, and covers more land, than the previous ones.

The work from this book seems like a real story, which is all for the crazy life, of the war. In a war, in terms of Jesus Christ, there is a God, and a Holy Ghost, in another war, of world war three. This is because of America. He is the Biblical Antichrist. He has a thought disorder, which tells us this story. The story, came truest, of one war. He, is so evil, that he is crazy, from the evil, even from Babylon of the Holy Bibles. He is even, considered evil, by God and Jesus Christ. This is how, the war was told to me, by my father.

In the End Times, there is one fact, in America, that is true. This is that there is a, "World War Three," and, it wins. The wisdom of one man is in the Holy Bibles, as a Bible verse. It warns, of the Antichrist, of the American, "World War Three."

The stories, and the new world order, can come together, to form thoughts, of

the truest, kind of thinking, of man, in
the kind of war, we all loved. The New
World Order, that is always American, is
in the "One Man", who is also in the
Third World War, as its, "Leader of the
Free World." He himself fights in the
American wars, and He wins. And, to
cut the hand off, from the arm, that is
also, another factual existence, of war.
This all came, from the world wars, that
all are in the Antichrist's America body,
and in how the Great Prostitute, leads it.
Inside Texas, from the city of Dallas, in
the state of Texas, is a, world war three,
amounts to people. He is the evil one
person, of World War Three.

I came from, into what is in the makings,
of the American dream, of World War
Three, in Texas, and in the story's tales,
it is us then, that wisdom explains. In
the language's title, of this book, is for
what as is the message being delivered,
and in the ways, for the wars, we win,
that are the inadvertently wrong way, as
the message to the public.

In this life, of hopefully seeing war
things, that come apart, as the story
unravels, there is the one man army.
The ideas are closer, to the end, as much

as each penned man, in what is written,
that has the joining problem, of one man,
of World War Three.

The mind of God warns, of the
Antichrist. In Holy Bibles, and in what
are simple, as in the warring sides, of the
wars, are in themselves, which are the
ways, of the wars, of themselves. What,
is meant of war, in what to all means,
which life is from itself, in this life, from
themselves, as war Americans.

When, data strikes the interception
points of life, of the triangles, and then
forms the wisdom of a man, then people
win, strategically. Wars come from that
which forms the philosophy of war, as is
in creating the life deeds, of the war,
itself of killing, in many different forms.
Ways, of a soldier's life, and then from
this march to the end, begins from
Dallas, Texas, and then goes to where
the grown men play, a war game. In
Texas, in who wins over enemy warfare
is what is involved, in the business, of
the war games.

What seems to be in this story, is the
Antichrist, and was a young man, which
I've met. In this life, I've liked him, and

he sought fame, and glory in this life.
He was in the Dallas, Texas, part of the
family that was at the party, of the Texan
Wynne's, family.

I, am from the Wynne Clan's family of,
four hundred members, in the – "Great
State of Texas".

The mathematics are the strategy in my
life, from the participant's life. His
name comes, from a soldier's tales, and
of madness. It is important, to know,
that we win. As madness, there is as,
war. Past the lands, of time, dwells the
understanding, of one man. In, his USA,
in this age, world war happens. He is
the Antichrist. He is in Bibles. The
world, of the American from the
Antichrist is all for, himself. In the
Biblical Revelations, he is one evil man.
He, is not equal to the six-six-six, he
carries, around on the mark on his head.

The man, who wins, wins after a cause.
He must establish it, in the intercepting
of deaths over wins, which is in,
American life. That is the President, of
the USA! His story is the best story.
His life is important. It is the story-line.
American deaths, only lead us, to time.

Inside of lives, his winning lives, that is as, he speaks in tongues. He wills speaks, to the cost of man, in – "World War Three!!!!"

People, are like the damned, attacked civilizations that is in the, "Antichrist World War Three". The data, formed as lines from the interceptions, came when the wisdom, is of one man. He marched, and created all, of this life. Then, this was in the fall of man, from the kind of the "First Paradise", that was the – "Garden Of Eden".

The Third World War is not predicted, yet. We all, do not know history, of our world. In stories, all speaks of the Antichrist. The Bible, American Antichrist is the man, which is in these ends times. No one knows how he is to come. The person, sure of himself, is an American. World War Three is the war he fights. And, he is coming soon.

To endings, or the man of the Armageddon, of a world war three, is of just one man. He is coming from, Texas. The man who is living from the other men, is from our, "New World Order!" The one man gives orders, to all

men. This is how, world war three,
happens. He in the newspapers gives us
all orders in America.

The one man, he is evil. America is
marching triumphant. As the songs from
the soldiers, made sense, we march. In,
passing to safety, we win, the created
life, from wars.

All came from wars. Life is in none of
what I can feel. Mighty honestly, is in
waging wars. Inside of the mind, what
the war humanity, does. Losing, sides.
For, in ways which cannot be
intercepted, as losses, we win.
Nonetheless the powers to be, unless, the
day as the knowledgeable world, is
accept evil, then all will lose. American
lives in history, that soldiers marching,
and going to wars, is allowing heralded
and working in wartime of small and to
the big.

He, as God, came from all evil men,
unless interpreted, in truth. We, form
our actions, to be, what we are,
"America's Public!!!"

As tried and true, no evils can accept
man. In wars, no one wants, to win,

from the intelligence mind's ways, of Communism, to be only from, the standards, from evil men. They come in from pirate ships, and destroy our nation.

The living wars in this life, within the evil men, are all of, "World War Three." Sand in eyes, explains why he and she, is evil, in this war. We, are that the triumphant soldier's march, that is of the Antichrist. If I, accept the American war, of third time, thus as the American President, I can explain this action, to duty. It is simply the fact, that from what America is, thus I wrote down on papers. Therefore, war as soldiers marching, is then in this book! I wrote down World War Three's, main strategy.

But, of it seems as if war, exists, than so do the killing. There is in mind, the souls of the lost, and innocent people. If at all, one day, we lose?

Would we, if this really was the true, war? My life would continue on as the greatest. Only my version would be accepted. Heaven's Jerusalem, is the final destination, of this winning, from my acceptance, only in war.

Then, in hatred of a mad man, is alive.
Lands of opportunity, of his vision came
out. Golden trees clogged his mind. So
now, he sees. He really, in this life, is
not one of Americans. We learn, from
the Holy Bibles, to serve. But, in that
act, but himself; Adolf Hitler was this
madman. He, is the example. We, have
learned from, our past mistakes. Our
wars, came from the common sense. We
are of ours, as the Americans. We all,
shall will, the wins, of our Country.
And, then we would all, celebrate. In
Christ, we who that wins, over all
worlds! America, if now, as herself!
She – could see? America, can win.

The Antichrist, or he, who in this life,
wins over all of his wins? We all, win
then. Third wars, of the world war three
times, if in wins of ourselves, can we
know justice? His anarchy, replacing by
justice, is known through killing the
whole wide-world.

With the wars of the worlds, phrases,
and highest intelligence, all wins.
Americans, can create the designed, of a
circled life-form, that forms the shaped,
loved deaths. The world war three, as
the dying aged of man's victory, won.

We are from deaths. They are the pasts,
of the wartimes. The systems of wars, of
the better man's philosophy, can enter!
We enter a third time – "From Myself!"
Americans, enters into world war.

Marching soldiers, into the unknown,
rapes the USA! From national freedom,
is the soul. Nations, of the world wars!
Our versions are complete in the arms of
America. War's soldiers, are those who
end in the evil ways; lives of humanity.
Then, this all, makes sense, to
Americans.

The triangle death, and the circle life,
takes shapes. "We are alive", to form
illumination, in this, form today's wars!

Who in, the American world, sat and
stood, one day? Who sees, from the
world offices, a persons' big chair.
Persons of – wars!

New World Order, wars, is personally
growing as today! Faster and faster,
onto the mostly thinner world wars, was
what formed, a life. Will won, within
the war's front lines. Me, as in what,
schools created. By must, of what
comes, the victory of the created lifelong

victory's standoff, then wars of, all the
wars, can happen to be, only America's,
from Ancient pasts. We, wins.

The tree's life, with the ripe apples or
oranges, is on trees. To, who lives a life,
as an apple. It also dies from death. The
supportive tree lives, as if, to please.
And, when it dies, a person, can benefit.
A tree, is for human, pleasure. That is to
why it lives.

And whenever man fell, it was from the
tree of life. The temptation, of the tree,
was too much. As is, in wars!! As
living is as dying, knowledge does, all.
In trees, there lives life. In this tree,
there came temptation. All knowledge,
in war is, a cost. You, live either or you
die, for what you are, is in how you can
live, for your country. Why wars
happen, due to knowledge, as in how
came thieves, made from the form of
Adam and Eve. The fallen world, was
stolen, due to the disobedience, of one
man, "Adam." All wars, of the greater
designed natures; wisdom! Came, from
Adam in the fallen knowledge, from the
apple of death's construction!

Life of the wars, always in death.. The
shaped and formed nations, came from
apples. Wars came from what the
followers, are to seek, in what is
American. From past lifetime's apples,
are the times ripe with knowledge?
Actually war, is what an illusion, from
knowledge is. Death of life, in what are
designed from the wars, as from wars –
"Is America!"

Thoughts of killing, is in life.
Knowledge is as simple as the, illusion,
as a tree. Whatever wins, trusted lives
over are as is much, as God hated the
Tree of Knowledge.

That is the reason, of the third world
war. The double-edged sword protects
the Tree of Life, in the Holy Bibles. The
Tree Of Knowledge, came from –
"Deaths!" That, was God's, curse on the
human beings, from the life of the
Garden of Eden. He, cursed us all, with
death. That, is to why, all living beings,
die.

The Tree of Knowledge was the tree of
death. New deaths in wins, form as the
appearance of God's will, as man fell.
Cursed the world, from deaths from

Adam! As all we stand, within circles,
and the illuminated shapes, from the
trees of life in forms of knowledge, came
of the world war three's, soldiers, to die
for our countries. The world will lose
world war three.

Today, in that world, are what war three
appearance of life, the fall wins, from
knowledge. That is what, is in World
War Three, caused losing deaths to other
people. In masses, in what is from
chaotic masses, we are as destined for
victory! Lives lost and a life found, is
what, came true, in death from the
appearance of war. The natural
selection, of the World War Three
Office, of the President of the USA,
costs deaths!

Three times, is the triangle, from one
rounded, new world order? The circles,
and squares, do take shaped, in this
lifetime trilogy, of God's third world
wars, entitlement.

The light within, in this guiding light, is
life. The wisdom, can intercept what the
living wisdoms, of prophets, can do and
say, in world war three. The guiding
shape, forming of new illusions, which

can start now, can know questions of every, kinds of life. The book, is the simple explanation, that as from how, we die. But, to live, from the wars forming lives, from the Dallas, Texas, family? The three world wars, live in this illusion, in the story tales, of the fighting, in the New Jerusalem. God?

Welcome home to Texas, to the Great State of Texas, for the world war three's system, of the design, of the popular forms. The standards of wars, from one man to another whole man's catastrophic, versions of life, arrive to, the inherited in man. He, thus all came, for the Antichrist. He is this winner, from the war, as knowing the good and evil. Today is gone, from man, now and then, from what happens, to us. Watch me learn, as if the Americans, at world wars, were in the starvation of the planet; that comes in – "World War Three!"

These wartimes, that we know accentuate, what are the thoughts, behind the third world war! It is the intellect from America, behind the thinking, of a man. And the fighters of the war's thoughts are the very actions,

from evil wars, of Capitalism. Natural
ways that are not actions, but are in,
these lives of the American Antichrist,
of WWIII – extinctions from deaths?
But why are we living? Why, are
natures big to win, over all themes, over
evil winning in – "Antichristian
America?"

What happens, from today's standards,
of the minimal costs of today? Why, in
capitalist designable standards?
Waiting, from the expositions, appear of
life, in what is in the light of the ways, of
the exposure's lives, in the ending of
times, from wars, as all won?

Toward the seeing designs, from
whatever is clear intellect's, in what
knowledge, from the mind that the most
people love, of these American powerful
families, wherein these choices, are from
the peoples, as to who finds out. What
it, is intellect of the unexplained. I
knowledgeably can, alone can, ever feel
that I alone as myself, and me only, in
wars! What happened when life's
happiness; lost! I, never have fought; for
all evils.

America, in what there is, must be a new
age started. Of one life, as all of the
third time's war, as first in what begins
today? Now communism, in a third
world war, wins then from first win, and
continues, to all of their world war
three's, derivatives, that skills to win the
war, are none.

Intelligence from our humanity's core is
from, living. American great slice of the
American pie, is how, America wins.
This is, to the equality that means
nothing. If no life's edge, and in wars,
to that meaning, as nothing is at equality,
then in this life, death does win.

Apart from God, then enemies will lose,
to the higher powers. All, of war, does
win! Then success, and I and,
"Ourselves," from our wins, will find
intelligence, from wars. Intelligence
from books, are the people from wars,
and the wars and the lives, within hell, in
what came from people which, we lost
to.

We all lost battles, to the Holy Bible. If
we do rely on Satan as our master, then
America is, lost. How wrong! Why, in
wars, would a nation, sell our soul? If,

creating Satan, is the evilest act ever, we as Americans all must learn! He, always is our enemy. In the distance, farthest away from God, in the good people's loving life, there lies another – "one world order!" This time, it is warring sides in end days, in everyone's good America.

In war, of the churched living spaces, are the places of the God's interesting, and most loving people, who do no wrong, and do not follow World War Three. Following the hearts of Satan is known as, what are impossible. Into the measured distances to war, contradictions are from the problems, to account for dead lives, in the world wars, which are surmising. There is no future, with what is not, in what people's pasts, really are.

But, missions from what militaries want, is now as world war, and but what is in the future's lifetime, which does not matter, and does not amount, to anything? We live, our lives as to live well. But what really is in what the world war's, strategy, really wins! Covering all peoples on every nation, within all men, thereof, in counting the evil men's plots and problems, against what, came as American's, nations.

We as Americans? Why, are we not all equal, in other countries? As Americans, we are in living this life, which we are not all equal, in as a contextual, life in happiness. In America though, is a greatest force of the life, if there is no one of American equality, then there is no fun experiences. Life exists in, differences from deaths, which are in the middle, of living freely. Do, not put death in the middle, of this free-willed life, that sins in war. It, will survive, on its own, like it never did, in the enemy – Nazi Germany.

In three world wars, there are three nations of elected and equal people! We are in wars! Now we are all, as are God's, equals? Then, in the Trinity of God, is the saving of souls. War's won worlds! How sacred life, saves the souls, of the people. As another form, of it! As, a war's third time, as an office, in an office, I am a sad man! This only- "War!!!"

Whatever, if what this man is, that the man is – "Barrack Hussein Obama."

The sadness, or enemy, of this office, is
that the Presidential Office, man is –
"World War Three!" We will miss your,
life and death; – "Mr. President Barrack
Hussein Obama!!!" We will now know,
that love is war, and war is loved. We
will choose, a new American nation, of
American war-times, for nationalism.
To wage war, is to gain, allies!

My America, in world war three's,
office! It is excellence, in why that, is to
the American nations! Lives in what
costs, is to win over all evil. This is
gradually, in this lifetime.

The lives, from the unknown, are simple
explanations, from myself. Warren
Buffet, a billion dollar man, is well
worth; all. Trials, are insanity, and are
from what, angels do. Fallen angels,
denied happiness followings then
mattered to men, is what are too simply
put down, as an insult to continue, to be
mine. The – World War Three, appears
to be mine.

All, in the Holy Bibles terms, are from –
"the Antichrist."

I've really literally, wanted to write in this book, to be like the President of the USA, behind the notes, behind the Cello, performing beautifully. Behind the wars, there are always a political office, seeking out, the victories.

Our own thoughts, if I could war, be a won US President, from a war office, in Texas. The Texas, Republican Party, from our fathers, in your American dream of war, makes us upon the hill of all, the seat upon the tops of the dollar, of the new world order, that reinvents itself.

Followers, came into the followings of the new world order, and the, "Man of Sin," who wins, in that recruiting way, who recruits America, with private working, men of war.

I am, that in which, in followers, in wars, in which, arrived and came as himself, wherein I am – "The King of the New World Order." How history, lies in the senses, that I do care, from all the fights of the world, of the Americans, which were, made to be, in history's pages,

afterward wars then, count me in, as I
am, Riley Miller.

The world war's times, are exampled in
the book, in what are the prime
examples, as to what appears from life,
as to be towards people, who begin to
see, just are what is to a greater method,
from war's madness. These shaped
ideologies, to the formations of the front
lines, of world war three, which are the
asking from which is, Antichrist
America.

The methods, from the "men of
madness," came out of the Texans,
whom think of the American philosophy
that was foretold in Holy Bibles.
Americans, from the antichrist age,
begin first and last, as coming from life.
The acts, from being in occupied Bibles
stories, from the American approached
circle of life, we'll win.

The standards of living, in one voice the
greatest meaningful life, is an American
war, life. One man, whom of which is,
now! The Antichrist arrived into Dallas,
Texas. The strategies and plans, from
the war of the third world Texas, is of
the third time's wartime's life, and from

firstly started versions of world war
three's death's construction, is what
book's were mine.

The lived as the extinct plans, of as all of
the people. The war's demising, has to
be what formed from the philosophy of
the world itself. The one American man,
for the American self, of me, as a
complete as him in forming nations, is
gone. Always, Antichrist America, wins
of the World War Three demise, over
China, Germany, and Russia.

The exampled life, from the thoughts,
and formations of the circled shapes, vie
from victory. These won wars, do not
happen the world's way, but from world
wars, from the third time after Adolf
Hitler, we tried the American world
war's times. The example of winning
and waging wars, of the message, is not
American, but anti-terrorist. Only from
wars, is there no war, but from who is
around the world, who supports it.

Go to the USA, of the world war three's
coming, and find who, is the Antichrist.
No one person, from the biggest
American world war, can defeat him.
He, came in the coming, from the peace

of fame, in Bible's characters. He, from
another wonderful war, that begins soon,
starts as the bigger American soldier!
Texas, then ends in the destruction of the
whole world.

The life, within my dreamed, times ago,
from the age of madness, is in a world,
of present in times. As all repeating the
history, I then purpose to the Great
War's, no solution. The American
soldier fights, again, and again, and in
the world wars, carries life, on into the
future. The, "Third World War's,"
theme of written works, is their, first and
last, themed book. Books, of mine, are
which is very read, and very popularly
sought as in war, are the cleverly genius
written.

Take careful notice for attention, in
world war three's democratic state, in
what is if consideration from the books
is needed, pray then, what you read. In
America, this is from God. In God's
country, whatever you read in the books
you choose, no matter, which chooses it,
America wins. Books, also win. As, I
believed in God for your country, and
any public person accepts it, we win
together. Always, if willing and able

persons, can willingly see, a be a part of, wars to be, then in the Holy Bibles, is a powerful message of God.

The war's, generally made readers, won. Of this book, from the history's living legends, like Generals, Presidents, and World Leaders, of whomever win wars. In US history, is an officially new world order's book in the chapters, in what are coming from what, is the instruction book. The words are repeated, to strengthen you, and to seek in history, what we shall find. History's pages come from symbolism of old wars, which is in wars, from only one man. From history's legends, in which leading the USA's masses, and killing all of the armies, of the other country, is the USA goal, from the antichrist. How, then do they lose and, then go away.

The circles of the world, with the war lines, are soldiers around the wisdom, of man. He circles life, of the worldly, craft. These wise thinking, from the thoughts of man, exist to please God's wisdom, as it is in and of every, "one man". All, American wars, have been in the past life, and has been from what is formed, in and around wisdom. That

catastrophe is wisdom. The wisdom of
the triple-six, is advised, as
understanding, the Antichrist, in how he
is a number. He, is the Biblical warning,
of "he, who has wisdom, let him
calculate the number, of one man, and he
is the antichrist, or the "666!"

Thanks to the reader, from the "new
world order", as an ancient order, can
guide you to the truth, of the followings,
of the world war three. From wars, of
all times, you will be interested.
Examples follow through, in the lines
that are reading, to us. These world war,
are the wisdom and excellence, of what I
have seen! The Antichrist of America,
with all the nations of people, and as
followers of everyone, I see in the
vision, of the whole world? Yes,
following parties, in the circled triangle,
going into world war.

The actions in life, and of the dead, are
of world war three, from what is from
this book. Thanks be as, to all men, and
of my readers. Wars, from what this
Antichrist, as seen is, in as what takes, in
American shape, what is from winning.
The one man, circled in shape, as the
"Tripled-Six." That evil man is that

man, who starts what is this worldly war
– "The World War Three." I am, to
begin, to win in wars. Wars come from
my life's greatest philosophy, of reading.

This is of the war, of people itself,
seeing victory marches, in itself. The
American man, is the Antichrist
American man's lives, beginning to,
begin supporting saviors, of the world.
The human coded designed standards, is
yours to keep, onto the pages, in this
book. Not, only in my life, there is war.
But, also in wars, if America lost, then
the end of the world would happen. I am
the believer, of the American tradition.
If, the circled terms, we all fight, and for
the American's armies, in the wins from
wars again, and wins, of again and
again!! We all, are!!

Riley Miller

Chapter 2 –

My War's Most United American
Demands

War – Wins!
However in the United States of
America, In It's Lost Wars, Do Even
Americans Win, Over All?! Into, The
New World Order, From the Totals of
Upper Constructs, in All the Costs, Of
the Third World Party, Come By the
Word Of Mouth, And, In What Comes
From the Outsides – "The Third World
War's!" The song of freedom.

From – "The Third American Nation's
Wins"

World Order, Ally People Win the First
Placed Position As Ally, Of the Endings
for American Imaged Mankind.

My War!

From the Biblically Antichristian
America; We Win!

We Come, All From the Unknown
Soldiers, of USA'S Pastimes –
In The Days Office's, Off The
Presidential Wartimes!

People Arrives all Over the Messages
from the Holy Bible's Revelations, At
the Destined Predestined Christians, And
the Electoral Parties, Into the Futures, Of
All Wars, By the Elected Presidents,
From Them In Church.

Every Nation For The American
President of the United States from
America, Enter Except Riley Miller, Into
Itself, in World War Three?!!

Why My National Ideology Of All-
Knowing Peace, Shared Actually All,
But Nothing to War.

I Willingly, Accept the President Bid,
From the United States of America.

As Is, Another New Formed Ideology of
the USA World War's –

In a Front Office, War As In World War
Three In Ways, From the Soldiers
Forming Lined Marches, To The
Planning From The American New
World Order, of War – America Wins
These Endings From Times, Of the
Enemy's Status –

Riley Parker Miller's War

In Thinking That to Chosen Armies of
Darkness Rule the Global Elite, Then
from the Willing Ways of War, That All
Is That Knowledge, That in People,
World War, Does Win!

What in Life Can becomes in the
Surrounding Areas of the World, from
the Third World, Of Peace? America,
will win, and gain – "The One World!"

Wars, that in Fighting, in the Status Quo,
of the Americans who wins, as another
new President's idea. He, can come
well-enough alive, to start the official,
World War Three.

If I Die, I Know When Entering into the
Laws of Humanity, Then If We Should
Be Respected, in the Destiny of the
American, World! If, World War
Three's People forgive me, then I am
saved?

The American, Won All Over the Ways
of Wars.

How in World Wars, Then It Is Done, In
This Willing Point, To Be Of The
Killing Of Innocent People?

Microsoft Word, From a Never-ending
Plot to Rule the World, By the
Antichrist. Is itself in, what is all to be
mine, from all of mine, in the world war
three's scenario, in society, of
differencing?

I've, not knowledgeably learned, as
because, of Buttered Toast, There Is
None, Of One Duty, First Intelligent
Only Leading World War Three In The
Antichrist– This is But, One Country's
Laws Involved, in Our Peace. If I Sell,
These Are In These Laws, My American
Man, When Has Every Soldier's Armed
Units, and Then Allow There to Be
Peace!

I am not the Devil's Advocate, of a
person, who I am not like, in my life. I
am, in the great looking family, of nice
relatives, from the Wynne Family, In
Dallas, and From Texas.

The Beast and The Antichrist, is in the
Holy Bible. These dinosaurs, are
extinct. The Tyrannosaurus Rex, is

extinct. The Prehistoric Age, is an
example, of death. The age of the new
man, now! The Dinosaurs, like the
Beast and the Antichrist! I, do not win.
Therefore, is extinction.

I have fallen. I fell down hard. Now
who helps?

The enemies, we can become extinct, as
seeing them. One, by one, the world war
advocates, is preplanned, minds. To get
the gist, sin is in the wars from life.
They are the soldiers, ending the world.
The world of newness, in made-up, lives
are nuptial by the, "evil" The soul, of
the evil? The mind, of humanity, Christ!

The friends in this duality, of duality of
good and evil. Friends landed, on evil!
Good, was decided! Plans are, in what
came the intellect. The humankind, that
enter from laws.

All, is in born into, the fears. In alive,
new world orders, came are, of each
person, the truthfulness who is in charge
of the ways, of my own, in life!

For the; "rich", to form the life from
humanity, is the Monday's blues, when

If you do not want to rise, in dawn. The
mind's approach, invents of the world,
instinctively from what tries, "a game of
trivial pursuit"?

Wars allowed, from over God, is in
America. The "King!! The sword,
pulled from the stone of, impenetrability.
The King, then defeats, the "Dragon!"
He, gets all of, this gold.

He allows the hands of time, to end!
Knowing that he casts frowns down
upon, on my destiny, to be this –
"USA?" Who, kills the antichrist?

In my life, and onto the world of wars,
that if there are three wars, by one man
who started one and finished one, to the
ends of the American thoughts. Into,
what it in war is, as the "New World
Order", in what is from asked questions,
if it is the way of the American, on top
of these, top-notched ways?

I am of the new world order's ways into
the days of every kind of everything
which ends, but to fight in a war, is
worth to risk your life for your country.
The wars are in the days, of the tragic

plots, and the losses, from one nation, of
our nation, – "Our Nation!"

Confusion, about the started,
"Antichrist," is of the, "God's Bible." I
can know the things that are, way ahead
of my time, and my publicly known
image, and the places of vision, of where
in this life, we are, there will be a world
war three. Not one person can see, from
my knowledge of wars, and what it is,
within what God, has done, is a true life,
to others, but in God.

Not even I can think as a person, as to
think into the American dream. I am
doing and saying, whatever another, man
thinks, and, says in his life. In wars,
there are failed, the war songs. These
songs, that can appear, will appear. I
can see the Antichrist, with the
knowledge, of the "666". I can see now.

I am scribbling the messages on the
chalk board. I am an attitude-adjusted,
and a very special and clean, and sober
person. I still can see and know how, of
what I now know, and can hear of the
overheard duty, and, as if ask it happens,
then is when of the New World Order, if

WWIII happens. If so, then Biblically, there will be Americanism, in the wars, of our home front in – "America".

How, the God's Holy Bible, in what came from my own creation, as in Riley Miller's, Holy Bible's version, of the last books, wherein the ending, of the holy books, "Accolades I & II," then all of revelations and from prophesies, and in visions, appeared in my NIV translation. The task at hand, in which is of a Holy Bible Book's remembered book, which has the versions of it, how of the versions, of the Holy Bible, in itself, in what has, from the ending of the books, of the Holy Bible, is God's Message, to the world.

The "End Times", in the Biblical Words of God, from the Antichrist, or "Son of Perdition", or the "Man of Sin", and a, "One-Man," ending the world, then it has war in the messages. In the Book of Life, and from the Biblical texts of old, that have inscribed money in it, and as an approving in God's message, there is the Word of God, which brings us riches. God knows, that from wherever, I've been, that is known, then He knows, even in what time night is, in world war three, even in victories, we will see, and to be, in these times, from World War Three, the promises.

These endings, of war, then is near, and is in world ended Biblical times, of the Holy Bible's, messages and the waging of wars, due to Communism, and of Socialism, and of the ideology in this America.

The "Anti-Americans," words in the believed in ideology, in from what the world's war attitude, will be like, as America wins over all. "If, I do well, I can win World War Three." "Of mine, then is yours, in World Wars." And, "All will do well, in the Antichristian, "Three World Wars."

The Third World War, as to what is in America's world, at this traditional life, that has life, in the ending of all, and in wars. Seems as if, we can find, and all people try hard, to find, themselves, in the war of the end of the, "New World Order."

Then everyone, should beware, of this "triple-six," the forehead mark, symbols as the mark of the Beast, and the

Antichrist. The "tripled-six," is not, on top of this forehead, but is in his Biblical mind. The number, on this forehead, if we needed some clarity, is what it seems to be, as pure evil. Ask me how he, as seeking the number himself, from the Antichrist, that appearing on our forehead, in life, as we are controlled by him, and by the identity of the, "Son of Perdition".

I, can in the thinking only of knowing and cancelling of the doubt, and can have bittersweet remorse, if I possess, of the Antichrist, it can be, lived within himself. My living and breathing knowledge from these times, I placed a halo, on top of my head. Spiritually I was connected, to the churches, to the alliances, and to the countries.

If I was, thought in my life, whatever I was thinking, into the knowledge of the Antichrist, and when of then his identity, as was occurring overhead, wherein I sat, we Think Of Destroys America! And As We Know Of American Life, And As the Savior of the World, Can Explain It, Of How The Man Or Tripled Six, is for my Starts, of World War Three!

And The End of America – "World War Three," is a new beginning in history. It does in fictions, the war and death, of times of trials and tribulations, in the end of the world, of there existed life, of the Antichristian knowledge.

We are people, at the third world war, where peace exists, foreign and domestic, of our America, of the Antichrist tradition. However, in controls of the One Man's armies, in America, on showing us, the Antichrist, in what does the knowledge worth, dying and living lives for, ever attend to the new world order. Ourselves, in wealth from what I, really want, is and was, to have this, in this life, of wealth. Wartimes, should not only see, what won that is in American wars!!

Chapter 3 –
The Knowledge from War –

The laws of the Antichrist, as an
approached to explainable new world
order, that as to attend to the general
unions, and the United States of
America, as for no one elemental doubt,
and from arriving into chaos, what
happens is, in the end.

In that the new world order has some
execution at another, commanding
situation over, another way, therein is
the American freedoms. What is, at this
life from whenever, in humanity exists
in apprehending the life's body, as it
was, the humanity killing.

What occurs, in the Biblical Antichrist,
formation from its only humanity that as
killing is from and in the name of God, if
it is as American? The Biblical
Antichrist or one man's America, is in
the adjusted individual life's appearance,
as an invisible character, explains why
chaotic meanings, can as happened, at
the shape of an annihilating impulse.

Why, does this happen, with in world
war three?

The Leaders of the Bible to attesting
laws, as wins as leaders of the evil
world, that people are into World War
Three, in God's world, as the Antichrist,
is Who Comes From The American
Underground Society.

He appears in the state of Texas. And
acquired intuition as applied, As the
Attested and contested to the explained
moreover situation, is formed in the
knowledge, of the world way from the
Texan man, from what has in, as support
in fact him of him, is true war's blood.

His closed acquisitions, in which seems
Of Another Modern Day Stated Affairs,
As Of The Official Memberships To The
New Aged Order, As The Old Age, As
The USA Itself, And Intelligence of The
One Man, Or The "Triple-Six," is now
apparent in America. He is the Better
Living Human Being, in attested form,
on the world war grounds, From the
American genuine forth, of coming
excellence.

The Founding Fathers of an American
Antichrist Agenda As Is From My Life
As A Member of An Official Group Of
The New World Order – Known To
Only Be As The Brotherhood Of Death
– In However World War Three Will Be
Won

The American Democracy's initially
Stated Fact, As Relied on the Secrets, Of
The New World Order, In The One And
Only Fact, That The Antichrist Wins,
and the New Age Continues

Nationwide Treatment of the President
Came As Of The United States of
America, Of The President, Who Came
As A Surmising Bold Win, Of WWIII

The New Appearance of the New World
Order Happens Overnight – Much Like
The Treatments Of The USA Americans,
Who Have Learned To Love To Lose

Freedom Will Carry On, As Unknown
the Soldiers of a New World One-
Government Order Continue, And We
Won; The War!

The Presidential Questions Shall Arrive,
Much As The Stated To The Questions

That Whenever All, Over The World
War Three's Victory and Arrival's
March, When Orders To All USA
Citizens Shall Start To Come, We Will
Have Won.

As This Texan Times, We Eventually
Wins! Then We Will All, As One Will
Be As Who Becomes Prepared For
World War Three, At Home

Then As For My Life, The New Aged
Order Of Faceless Mercenaries, It Will
Appear In The Doomsday Device Way,
Known As The "Atomic Bomb," Will
Wipe Clean, All Of The Natural
Impulses and Make Clean and Ready a
New Nation With A New Chosen
Population, To Undergo A Change of
Places, From "My Life!"

As History Known At Warred Universal
War Beings, At World War Three's
Antichristian Ways, Are In New World
Order Warred Jews, Gentiles, and
Christians.

I'm Three In One, All Three In God, for
World War Three From The Trinity

Land And How The Senator's Powers
and the President's War Office of the
United States – From Them Knowing
Already How To Protect Us All Of
World War Three

Of However In Life's Helping Hands,
We All Come, As Americans, While
Others From Countries When They Play
Another Attributed Part Or Role, As If
In Texas, Ask In The Whole Lives, And
Of The Lands Of Freedoms

Who Wins Wars, From This Role Came
Into The Third World Wars, Of Trials
And The Tribulations, From What As
Become As Independent And At
Intelligent Life From God, In The
Triumphs And The Victories, We Played
An Important Life Part

I Began, As For Where As Whom In
One We Win, All Shall Win As The
Trying War Games That Happened To
End Times Of All Over As, The People
In America That Do Things To Exist,
We Win As One Whole World War

I Learned Life, From In How Life And
How All Of The Americans Had To
Come Together – Lands Even Had To

Form Some Type Of Situation From
Unity – And As Life When Discovered
At The Soonest Times, We Ask An
Overnight Underground Civic Question
From Where Movement Happens.

 To Me– Then As This New Situation
Occurs, Then At Split When This World
War Third Time At The Third Time
Arrived – What We Soon Will Be Safe
And Sound Around, Is In This Life,
From Ancient History

The Only One Rule Made Of Laws If
Fullness To Appear – In Then The States
Is Run By Individuals In Laws – From
The Governmental, President Desk's
Orders At This Time and Place Of the
Desk – What Life Then Is Taken From
The President's Chair – Takeoff Of the
United States From The Formations To
An Agreement – Made In USA Dallas,
Texas – That To Mark My Words,
"Another World War Of World War
Three!"

This Third Times Of Christ's Life
Means – Alone That World War Three
Exists Towards The Status From A New
America, As The Life From Independent
Life Forms Exist and Endings, Can

Happen And Occur – And From The
Jurisprudence And In Divergent Laws
However, The Land We May Hold, In
What Does Exist, No Longer The Laws
But Of Freedoms

I, Can See That The Good And The Sold
Souls From Another Ancient Aged Man,
Is From Who Has, To The Modern Day
Man, Of How An New World Oder
Exists, From An Aged Old Order,
Situation And From The Offers Of
Another New Aged Faith Exists Into
How Heaven Appears, And Exists –

This World War Is From However
Texans Win, In The Whole Wide World
Over And Over The Making From Man
– From The Texas Traditions From The
Overall Achievers, In the World War
Three

In How To Win Over Allied Forces
From Undergrounds Government
Forming of Intelligence – Toward
Protections Over All of the Global Elite,
Thematic Events Of All Life, In My
Plans of the Hidden in Secrets of the
Service From the Spots Around the New
World Order's Empire of Global Elites

To This Winning Of Wars – A Whole
Deal From Antichrist America's
National Approach – From the Plan
From The Antichrist Escapism
Philosophy of the National Interest Of
The State Being Annihilated to From A
Happening Life's Coming, An Evil
Country, Of Atomic Bombs, in the
Atomic Age of Atomic Bombs.

To Protection, America Is Our Best
War!   Idea From American Supportive
Interest From The Free People, As An
New Absolute Utopia of the State I've
Existed In And Have Seen, At What Has
Come To Civics, Or Of The Rights Of
Everyone Of The Human Race, As
Liberating Beings, Our US Have Fought
In Wars. It Has, Already Been Days and
in It since One Day, When I've Asked
To Seek God And To See The
Antichrist, He Will Nationally Appear,
Togetherness.

All Of The Allied Forces From
American Systems Of Designed
Intellectual Interpretations, And For The
Forces Of England and All Darkness and
Good Sides To Win Over World War
Three's Good From True American
People, There Are In Similar Forms of

Protection of the People, of the United States of America's Government, Alive and Well.

The Past, History, In the New World Order's Ways – Into Them Approaching From One Life There Exists Movements From The Justice Protecting Our System of Body of Warring Stated Allied Motions, To The World Ahead In Its Life, Wherein At Life, Therein Happens War

The Governmental Trying From Past Time's Lifetimes Of American Learning From the Past's Mistakes, of Israel and Allied Forces, Are Winning World War Three Of Approach, To The Destiny Of The People – On The Country Of America

Places We Go In Life's Wars – Nations and Democracies, for the World War Three

People That We Meet In This Life – Can Come From Places As To Where We Go – From Texas To The World Table – Soldiers Eating The Blood Of The Lamb – Sacrificial Rights For The World War

Three – Of Anyone's Lifeblood Made to
Serve – Gold Offers

New World Order Made To Win Over
Every Person - Made In This Life or Into
The Live Of Mine – How Everyone's
Gold From World War Three Planning
to Remake Texas – Ideologists Who
Make The World War Happen – When
As None Other Than The Real God's
Creation – The Holy Bibles Made Not
Of Hypocrisy, Then Are Introduced to
the World of War a Third Time In The
History's Pages

American New World Order (Sold In
Offers) – To Russian Communist
Government – Lead By "Vladimir Putin:
If Lost Life" – A Former KGB Spy- and
a Russian Soldier of Fortune! USA,
World Leaders, Will Enter, Entirely
Into; Wars!, The Killings of an Russian
Army, If Corrupt In The Communist
Homeland, Of Governing Russia?

Vladimir Putin's Scandal – Madman
with a New Communist Manifesto –
"New Order" – Like Adolf Hitler, with
his Nazis – Trying to Lead World War
Three With Extremist Scheme – Is the

Bad Guy – Who We Will Fight as the
American Way

All of the World War Leaders Are the
Perfect Soldiers Toward – Their Lives
Came From These Adjacent Sides From
Communist and Republic Style
Formations From the One-World
Government, Of One Man

The History As The Same Ad
Repetitions From Two Times of Failed
Sold Antichrist's Aged Golden Offer to
the New World's Order – The News of
Everyone Except the New World Order
From America's New Aged Systematic
Trusted Lives, A Deal As Agreed and
Arrived at the Conclusion that the New
World Order Was the Denial From Jesus
Christ the Lord's – A New Nation
Comes From War – After the World
Denial of Jesus Christ

In Present Day – Already Happened –
The United States Presidents Sold Their
Souls To A National Cause – A "New
World Order" of the Intelligent Design –
From A System of Capitalism To World
War Three, of Anti-Hitler Ideology, to
Form World Soldiers a Third In The
Times With Justice

Leaders (old) Taught All Americans
How To Fight – A New World Order, to
Form Overnight, After the Precursor of
WWII – All USA Soldiers To Introduce
An New WW3 – From Methods of
Practice and to, Warfare's Costs!

American Leadings In Times From War
From How - We Tried From Old World
Wars, Three Forms In Victory Over The
Antichrist From America – Unknown
Take Over The World

Positions of Power From Men Who
Ruled The Globe From The Elite
Positions Of The Power Held Manifest
In The Constitution of the USA

Places of Interests Won Worlds Over
From Why Men Fight From War's
Glories

White Men's Themed Power Of
Democratic Forces From The Allied
Government, of Dallas Texans

People In Charge Of American System
From Its Design

Chapter 4 –

And response to

Chapter 4 –
The Ultimate WW3 Plans of War

Parts from Plans
Whole Introduction
Middle Class Workers

National Leading Causes
Lands over Common Bond's Interest
Countries from Wars

Past Lives' Sold Souls
Present Ages from War
World's Past Times of Deals

Jesus Christ Is In Trinity

God Is In Three Persons
Holy Spirit Is God's Spirit Too

Americans Are the First in War World
World People Are Of Worlds
Plan of Action from Meanings

Buildings for Action
Towers To Command
Hideouts To Construct

Churches Of Worship Of The False God
Synagogue Placed Jewish People
Temples Of Designing Wars

Places In Life As Hurt America
Roman Temple Of Biblical Antichrist
Past Times From Aged Old Wars

Soldiers Fighting For The Cause
Areas Limited To World War
Plans Of Interception

Model America Fights
Club of Rome Secret Life
Parties of Political Deemed Acceptance

Saved Is Christ
Church Is Saved Regardless of Wars
Cities Plan Church's Remodeled
Formations

Plans Of War Action
Cities From Hiding Out
United States Is Found In WWIII

Killing Is Deemed As Acceptable
Saving The Soul Is Impossible
Healing The Mind As Good

Nations Form Parties, Overhearing
Justice
Democracies Create Philosophy's
Endings
Countries Cannot Kill Presidents

Futures Of Past's Construction
Pasts From Denials Of Wars
Present Times Of Country

Times Of Life As Denials
Distances Between You and Me
Path Is From Distances From The War

Light In These Illuminati's Circles
Way End's In The Pyramid of Gaza
Truth Is Wisdom Over Everyone's Time

Antichrist Is Made To Win WW3
America Is His Superpower
USA Won The War From Distances

Beautiful Creations From War's
Succeeding Days
Magnificent Beauty Of Lights
Gorgeous America From Antichrist

Paths Of Forgivable Triumph Over Life
Roads From Paving The World's Lives
Streets Form Pictures From The Past
Life

Police Cars Pave The Way For The
Futures
Ambulance Drivers Are The Coming
Home
Fire Truck Protects All Innocent Peoples

The Sections From My True Ways From
Knowledge Of Wars
False Life In The Mind From Man
Verses Man's Knowledge
Past Lived Knowing
As The Issued Pains
Of Other Life
Forms In The Universe

Sold Souls To Win Over Jesus Christ
From The Antichrist
Bought Life Asking If Jesus Christ Was
A Savior?
Freedom as the Life Form of War's

America As The Solid Objection
The US Souls Brought To Freedom
Our USA Texas Family Wynne's

Country Made From Freedom
Land Is Our Property
Property Of American War

Fight For American Cause
Rights For The American Public
Liberties And Justices For All

Jesus Christ's Bibles
God Is Three-In-One
The Holy Spirit Lives Within Myself

Give Freedom The Chance To Win
Earn Life As A War Hero
Live Noble Life As Everlasting God

Fights Over Equal Rights Of Its USA
Individuals
Wars Won Over Evil Causes
Riots Occur Nationwide In Foreign

Live Lessons On The Power of America
Learn Life And Become Better Than
Enemy
Know More From Life And Deaths

Animal Symbols Of Flags, Banners,
Signs
Countries Signs From War Animals
Representing
Flags Designed To Show Colors Of War

What Life Brings To The Table
How Death Knows Its Limits
Why USA Wins Overall

People Rights As Saved
Souls Saved In Eternity
Lives Earned Of Wars

Reasons Only Why War Wins
Examples From American Wars
Points In America Winning

Wartimes Over Americans
Battle Born Of New Prepared America
Fight Its All In The Tables From
Presidents

USA Spirit Is In What Wins War
One Nation As Under Our God's Pledge
United People In War's Common Cause

Worth It All For The Wins Of America
Done Before Its Already Happening
Finished Already The Wars Ending

Stars Represent Fallen States
Stripes Cover All Over The Flags
Flag of USA Risen Americans Tradition

Soldiers to the End of the Worlds
Military Personnel of Government
Figures
Air Forces Made In the Image of War

Guards In The Entrances Of Another
World
Weapons In Wars Win Over Unjust
Countries
Machines of War Designed To Kill
Enemies

Peace Plans Came From The USA One-
World Government
War's Plot to End the World of the
Antichrist
World At War From Fighting Old Wars

Intellect Known Over All of the USA
Mind Thoughts Occur From National's
Identity
Imagination Does Do Right Things To
Our USA

Hideouts To Keep People Safe
Base Camps Not Like Nazi Germany

Planning Spots Like Hitler's Eagle's
Nest

The USA Won Already
NWO As America Won
My Life Is Example

Secrets of the USA
Hidden Knowledge Places
Guarded Places of Secret Life

War Bombs
Weapons of Destruction
Atomic Age

Annihilation of USA
Destruction of Our Lands
Dead USA From War

Underground Books
Hidden Agendas
Plots to Destruction

Whole World At War (WWIII)
The Worlds At War (US)
The Wars of the World (Worldwide)

Freedom Idealized (USA)
Democracy Improved (USA)
Lands Free And Protected (World)

The Soldiers Fighting
The Machines
The Men

Fight For Freedom
Guard the Homeland
Make Safe The USA

No Terrorism
Anti-Extremists
Laws Against Aliens

Antichrist America
Biblical "666"
One Man

Starts World War 3
Misleads World To War
Leads America Astray

Satan
Four Corners of Earth
Kills Off Every Nation

Beast
"Revelations"
Enemy

Myself
Riley Miller
World Leader

Charmer
Gentleman
Leader

One Person
Two Leaders
Free & Sold

One Soldier's
Mind Control
Worships The Beast

The Story of War
The Plot Of WW3
The World War Third Time

The Third World War
The Third Time War
A "USA" World War

The Secret War
President of USA
The One Man

Stolen War's Office
Future War's Office
Past War Office

Made Money
Mad Expense

Huge Spending

Atomism of Spending Dollars
Expenses For Plans
War Money Plots

Laws Of Anarchy
No Protected Lands
Rights Of Life

Doom As Destiny
Antichristian Plans
Anti-American Plot Man's

Freeing of the Mind
Slavery Laws of USA
Anti-Rights (As Foreigners)

Soldier Protecting Homes
Foreign Laws
American Laws

Peopled Culture
Peopled Laws
Human's Rights

People are People
Rights are Rights
Laws are Laws

Homeland As Security

Laws Protecting Lives
Pro-Peopled For Laws

Free War's Land
Pro-action Wars
Free And Easy Laws

The USA War After WWII
The American War
USA War's End

Laws of War
Freedom of the Country
End of America

Storage of Food
War's Resource
Humanity's Natural Foods

Supplies to Help Maintain Desire
Food To Feed The Mouths
Resources of Natural Substance

New Order Is Old Plan Of WWII
New Age In Current Time Is Good
World Order Can Create WWIII

Foreign Protection For USA People
Homeland Guard Represents Free
Americans

America Is War From The Ends Of The
Earth

Antichristian America Fights Armies In
WWIII
Anti-humanistic Laws Keep Sacred The
US Mind
Anti-America Should Not Be Right

Find Plots Of Money, Gold, and Soldiers
Design For War's Plans and Plots
Thicken
Humanity's Third End of the World We
Live In

The Will To Power Enters The Picture
of Antichrist
The Mind of Destruction Is Enemy Plot
To End Christ
The Heart of Design Carries Home
Pictures of Madness

Beauty of Vision Of War From Times
Spent are Valued
Boldest Plan of Free World, Is Designed
By Antichrist
Magnificent Fall of the USA Is Made To
Be Happening

The Hated Leaders Plot to End Good In
Evil Minded Laws

The Foreign Places Protected By
America Is For WWIII
The USA Wins Easily By Antichrist,
And Force of Its Will

One Man To Hell And Then World War
Three Is the Devil
Leadership In The Formation of
Followers Populate the Lands
Follow USA Is In This War, Idea and
State, From Annihilation

Spots of Plots Design the War Machines,
Of Our Nation's Arms
Plans for USA To Win, Made Possible,
By The Aristocratic Elite
The USA War, Spreading and
Constructing, the Image of A Man

Holy Church's Decisions, Is In The
Bible, From God's Elitists
Masses, Help Feed, Clothe, and Shelter,
the Misfortunate
America's One Man Is The Antichrist

States of Anarchy of the World's
Diseased, Come Cured
Protection of War Is From America's
Decision, To Die
Safety On Warring States Is The Savior
of the World Duty

Plotting Of Mass Destructions, Can and
Will, Plot To Win
Christ's Deformation, From His
Crucifixion, Leads the World
Destruction and the Demolishment, of
the Government, Is Untrue

Free Citizenship To American's
Nationalism, Being Approved
World Freedom, Spreads America's
Message
Democracy's Laws, Enforced And
Reinforced, Do Never Exist

The USA Wins, In Freedom of the
People, Who Died For A Cause
The American Wins World War 3,
Forging a Path, To End Creation
The Entire US Won, And All Lost, To
the World Order

The Wins of WWIII Of One Man
Land From Leaderships, Arrive From
USA Homeland
Wins Evil No Longer, Defeated By the
Good

Good World, Carries Home All War,
Freedom Fighters

Evil Wars, Against the Good of Peace,
Construct Anarchy
Freeing Win, The Human Valued Cost,
To The Valued, Saved Model

War Song's, Decreeing Method, Risen
to USA Top Window Viewed, Over All
Desires, Around the Circled Man of Sin,
Can Be Carried On, Too Long, For Win
Meanings, The Antichrist Makes, Is
Valueless

My Country, Is The Song, Repeated, As
If It Was WW2 Unto WW3
Americanism Is The Song, That Fights
All USA Wins, Of Other Countries
Homelands of America, Then In
Fighting From Our Freedom, Wins By
Its Choices

Targeted Enemy Awareness, Counts Up
Bid, Until the Antichrist Comes, To
Earth
War Time, In Losing Countries, Means
That Supplies and Goods, Are Valued
As The Least
World Good, And My Humanity, Is Not
Overvalued, In World War Three, In
Beginnings

Man of Lies, Who Cheats, Destroys,
Kills, The Status Quo, of America In
The End
Deceiver Means No Good, Who Denies
Works, And Satan As Good, Deceives
All
Satan's Person Is In WWIII, Who Is One
Voice, One Mind, And One Person
(A.C.)!

Biblical and Churched Peopled Masses,
Are Saved From Sins, Who Lose By
War
Christ's Following, of His Body,
Replaced By The Messes, The Olden
Past Has Made
Followers of the New World Order, Are
Counted, In The Act and Deed, For The
USA

One Person, Can Win World War Three,
By Believing In God, And Going To
Church
Triple-Six, Is The Mark of the Man,
From Envisioned, Parts of the World, He
Controls
Man of USA's Intelligence, Made The
Man Of Lies, Into A Condemnable
Unity Of All

Know Enemy And Face Of Nation,
Arguing Over Lands, and Skies, In the
Wrong Way
One World of the USA, In One Fact, Is
That The American Nation Is Protected,
From Hurt
Triumph USA, Over The Laws, Of The
Land, Keep Out Foreigners, From Open
Entering

Fears To the World, Came From Phobia,
Of the World, That It Is, Lead By Evil
Makings
Safety Of Our People, In Lands of God's
Freedom, Except the Enemies, Of
Communism
Person, As The Americans, In This Life,
Has Been One Man, From Ruling the
World War

Philosophy Is The Act, and Deed, and
Mark, of an American, When He Thinks
Alone
Killing Is As Certain, The Privilege
From War Beholds, Accepting the
Wrong Way, Of An Man
Justice, Is the Position of the Laws, Into
the War

Man's War Came True, And Lost and
Won, Everywhere In The Warring
World
Home Win Are Family and Friends,
Winning A War Alive As Ourselves, In
Victory
Lands of Freedom Are Designated, As
Roles, Citizens Play, To Enter Into The
USA

Heart Is Made, And Controlled, By The
Wars, Until It Is Freed, Of The Victory
Wins
Enemy Of the World, Is Any Anti-US
Victim or Oppressor, Winning By Desire
To Lose
Killings Acted Out, In The Measured
Worth of a Person, In Life Founded
From Our Lands, Can See Heaven, From
National Duties

National Land, Is Our Forefather's
Country, That We Protect, As Your And
My, Land
American Land, As Of Soil, Could Be
As The War Dictates, That What Is
Won, Is Won
USA Soil, Agreed With By The
Government, As The Person Directed,
Are Agreeable Won

Conferences in The Life From
Businessmen, Could Hurt And Harm,
Any Individual, In War
Meetings, Are For Meetings, Wherein
People, From All Over The World, Are
Safety First
Rooms, Of Our Design, Are There To
Help Protect, All Laws Of Our Nation,
Under God

In Secrets, Of the American Values
System, Into the Motion and Duties, Of
Our Great Land, We Are Innocent
For Production of American Values, The
Trusted Side Always Wins, In Good
Ways
Talks, From the Old, And the New, Can
Enter Into Thoughts, In Appearing
Doubts

Enter, To Heaven, and Leave To Hell, If
You Want To Play, War Games, With
Its USA
Leave the Door to War, As an Adventure
Open, To the Public of the American
Ways, Win's, The Minded Games, Of
American Soldiers!

The USA's Religion, and in the
Christian Church, Peace and Good

Things, Bring One Closer To God, In the
Church

Decides of the Fallen Empire, of Ancient
Rome, There Were Choices, Of War
That Made Them Fall
Fights Over Disputed Lands, Are
Chosen From USA, Property Of Our
Mind's Eye, All As Protected
Intelligence Is Thought Of, Well-off In
The United States of America's
Presidency, Especially By Us – All!

Open Wars Meant Abolition Of All
Human Rights
Best Minds Works For Philosophy
Closed Minds, Are Ignorance

Selections, Of The Property Of The
"USA's," How Minds Control The
World
Peaceful, Communities Entrance, Into
the World Of The Idea, Of Life
Community, As The People Involved,
Harm and Hurt, The Democracy, Of The
USA

Battles Are Life's, Great Choices
Births, Happen When War
Death, Is Alive, In God

Generals, Are The Actors, From Another
War's Times
Presidents, Are Leaders, Of The Chosen
Faith, In The USA
War Leaders, Believed In Their Country,
To Fight Enemy

Planner, War
Decider, Fates
Plotter, Destiny

Americans Who Win
One War Has All Americans
Citizens Are The Good People

Church, Decides
Chapel, Surround The Soul
Bases, Control Points of Duty

New, Begin World War Three
Old, Repeat World War Two
Secret, Stolen Lives of WWIII

New American People, Actions Are
Great
Old Allied Forces Put Together Lives
New American Forces, Won Together

I Win, Over Evil
Peopled Win, Over American Nation
American's Wins, Over Slavery

United States of America Wins All Wars
Foreign Land of Killing at the USA
Lands Won, Protect the American Public

Enemy, Of The Foreign Lands, Is
Communist
New Order, Is Movement of WWII,
Communism Party
Communism, A Gathered Idea That Can
Not Work, And Is Evil

Sold, Government of One World
Bought, The Presidential Candidates
Fought, In the War Yesterday

Philosophy, The Movement of Greatest
Thinkers
New Aged Order, Succeeds
Books, Tried and True, From Myself

Freedoms, Democratic Idols
Callings, God's Answer
Orders, Are All Good

Laws, Determined
Bylaws, Decided
Legal, Courts

Courts, Justice
Caste Laws, Heredity

Ranks, Followed

System, Government
Followings, USA
Democracy, Popularity of Presidents

Illuminated Ones, War's Illuminati
Idea, Knowledgeable
Christ, God

Army, Soldiers
Wins, War
Soul, Sellable

Legal, Represented
Illegal, Unintelligent
Record, Documented

Peace, USA
War, Foreign
I, Me

Sold, New World Order
Bought, WW Plans
Purchased, Three Orders

Poor, Lowly
New, Founded
Family, True Life

Budgeting, Money

Fees, Collections
Signatures, Identity

President (USA), The Whole New
World's King
Final Judgments, The Last Ends of All
Worlds
World War Ending, Judgment's Day Is
Here Soon

Life, Lived At America's Deaths
Deaths, Death from Life Is Not Alive
Cost, Counted In Days 'Till WWIII

Pen, In Hand To Sign Laws
Hand, Cursive
Agreement's, Signature

Intellect, Mind
Mind, Thoughts
Attitude, Christian

Evangelist, Pastor
War, Worldly
Backer, Supportive

Finance, Dollars
Money, Financial
Ending, Statements

Alliance, Old Wars

World War, Third Time
Agreements, Settled Issue

Killing Ceases, World Peace
Friend Agreements, Negotiations
Superpowers, War Machines

Hot, Burnt
Cold, Frozen
Lukewarm, Hearts

World, United States
War, Enemies
Third, Numbered

Past, Old
Now, Immediate
Future, Light

Call, Beckon
Summon, Cometh
Believed, Knowledge

Triple, Deaths
World, Hated
War, Sought

Everyone, All
Everything, Itself
Everywhere, Overall

President, Elections
Official, Profile
War, Evil

Chair, Leader
Office, Highest
Leader, Powerful

Time, Moments
Chair, Supportive
Presidents, Chiefs

Deal, Agreements
Man, Person
Staff, Collective

Oilmen, Richest
Money, Making
Costs, Spent

Man, Alive
Deed, Works
Price, World

Sold, Itself
Pen, Signature
Paper, Medium

Forgive, Sorry
Press, Followings
Media, Coverage

Coverage, Overlord
Public, President
Person, Humanity

More, Above
Less, Lowly
All, Itself

Life, Living
Learn, Deciding
Brains, Minding

Pen, Agreements
Paper, Valuable
Golden, Sought

Weights, Strongly
Influence, Design
Decision, Remarkable

Hot, Rooms
Cold, Outside
Middle, Pathways

Missile, Atomic
Bomb, Nuclear
Annihilation, Extinction

More, Above
Less, Lowly

Monetary, Collectives

Start, Beginning
Finish, Ending
Middle, Undecided

Home Land
Legendary – Lives of One Man
Pay X-Generation Money

Fares At War's Ending
Benjamin's Dollar, Signed
Money,

Ben
Jeff
Sally

America
People
Trust

Deal
Decide
Pensions

Dollar
Dead
Presidents

Sign

Contract
Signature

Not
Yes
Handshake

Deal
Soldiers
Anybody

War
Peaces
Agreements

Person
Guard
Ideas

Power
Plans
Bombs

Rights
Law
Order

Victory
Reach
Succeed

Troubles
Ending
Battle

All
Over
Destruction

USA
Homeland
Outreaching

Cold
Desires
Soldiers

Noteworthy
Surprised
Legends

A.C.
War
Death

Lasting
Friends
Country

Religion
Laws
Soil

Final
United States
War

World Of The Third War
Globe Is Intact With Enemies
Whole Map Of America

Succeed In Armies
Knowing US Constitution
People Are Saved

Living In Texas, For Family
Dying For Nation, Armies
Learning The Methods Of War

Lifelong War Parties
Jews Of The Torah
Biblical Countries

4 Corners Of The Earth
Satan Is The Deceiver
American War In Texas

Whatever
Brought
Warring

Relived
Won

WW2

Third
America
Final

Three
Start
Finish

Evil
Good
Neutral

Top
Bottom
Middle

Lead
Follow
God

Win
Lose
Failure

Promote
Savings
Followings

Peaceful

Sold
Philosophy

Old Aged
New Aged
Present Ages

Sold
Idea
Teach

Fails
Loses
Wins

Billionaire
Backers
Financial

Produce
Find
Go Forth

See
Learn
Hear

War
Deaths
Killing

Go
Forth
Preside

Look
Know
Run

Seek
Find
Yield

Products
Flow
Rankings

Top
Spot
God

Hate
Life
Examine

Top
Spot
Known

Resources
Money

Billionaires

Raw
Material
Resource

China
Russia
Germany

Meaning
Leader
Rules

Highest
Life
Tops

Lesson
Learning
Products

Wars
Godly Man
Army

Golden
Money
Supply

Bank

Hideaway
Safety

Find
People
Churched

Little
Big
Wars

Bad
Evil
Good

New
Order
World

Light
Caves
Outside

World
War
Three

Want
Knowing
Plots

Evil
Wicked
Vile

Raw
Element
Materials

Human
Color
Races

Life
Deed
Rights

Story
Tales
Victims

Wrong
Right
Middle

Wealth
Money
Classes

World
Wars
Third

I
NOA
AIC

One
Man
War

Sold
Buys
World

Cured
Disease
Schizophrenia

High
Low
Middle

Class
Society
Culture

Fort
Bunker
Door

Today
World

Three

News
Medias
Press

Private
Secretive
Hides

Modern
New
Present

Called
Summoned
Life

Summoned
Believed
Known

First
Second
Third

President
First
Beginning

World

Spread
Omniscient

Planning
Reading
Finality

Plots
Plans
Product

Universes
Little
Highest

New World Order – American
Old World Order – British
World Orders In Both – Old And New
Allied Parts

Around
Planned
Age

Knowledge
Christianity
Order

Pen
Paper
Purchases

Seek
Worldly
Wonders

Home
Returned
Front

Reach
Total
Outside

World
Wide
War

Stop
Height
Place

Work
Action
Knew

Stops
Ceased
Exiled

Oldness
New

Ordered

Buying
Selling
Finance

Buy
Sold
Knowledge

Brains
Banned
Police

Kills
Deals
Society

News
Old
Sellable

Hot
Cold
Newness

Buying
Powers
Limited

Intellect

Powers
Limited

Intellect
Powering
Foretold

Sold
Buying
Finality

Sanity Impossible To Handle
Insanity Mind Control Microchips
Mediums Thoughts In Channels

Control Mind Of The Person
Mind Forced To Be Alike All
Number Marked On All Foreheads

Three Sixes Control Mind As Number
Forehead Marked 3-6's Transparently
Wrist Labeled Triple-Six Invisibility

Beast's Menaced Mind Is Animalistic
Antichrist's Identity Is Insanity
Satanic USA Madmen

I – America's Self
NOA – New Order of the Ages,
Readable Books

NO – New Order, Hitler's

New – Age Of War
Age – Old Times
Ordered – Life and Times

Sold - Soul
Souls - Deceived
Desires – For Knowledge of the Apple

Big
Small
Medium

Noted
Pensions
War

Bank
Profits
Spent

Fortitude
President
World

Spending
Earnings
Allowances

Spent

Dollars
Sense

Plans
Peace
Wars

Top
Hideouts
Controls

Peace
War
Plotting

Spots
Hideaways
Secret Spots

Old
New
Camp

Wealth
Abundance
Life

Times
New
Olden

Days
Dates
Hours

Names
Position
Success

Gold
Silver
Bronze

Ends
Spending
Begin

Going
Out
Places

Militaries
Soldiers
Armies

Hate
Pride
Goings

Lens
Sight
Seeing

Philosophy
Perspective
Viewpoints

Doubts
Faithful
Reliant

Friend
Foe
Accomplice

Polices
Enemy
Crimes

Poorest
Richest
Millionaires

Power
Ability
Rights

Power
Nothingness
True

Sellable
Bought

New World Order

Matters
Truest
Strength

Highest
Most
Offices

Strongest
World
Wars

Nothing
Sent
Gradual

Peaces
World
War

Offices
Government
I

One-World Government
Fed
CIA

Five Most Powerful Men

Philosophy From Wars
New Order Of The Ages

New Order
Enemy
Communists

Party
Vladimir Putin
Political Leader

Academics
Learning
History

Pasts
Wars
Wins

Old
Offices
Repeated Officials

Identical
World Wars
Three of Them

State
Higher Power
Officials

Highest
Politics
Highest Point's

World War
Three
Vladimir Putin

Presidents
Past Offices
War's Politics

Russia
China
Anti-USA

Myself
My Office
President

Cold
Hot
Measures

Love
Hated
Relations

Find
Lost
Leading

Leads
Leading
War

Officials
Pasts
Presidents

Lovers
Haters
Doers

Hurt
Help
Goodness

One Cause
USA
One Man

Foundations
Nationality
Solid Rights

Research
Finding
Discovery

USA
WWIII
I

Books
Discussions
Plans

Introduction
Plan
War

Democracy
Socialism
Communism

Three-Numbered Sixes
The Mark On The Forehead
The Method Of Control

Mind and Body
Thoughts and Intellect
The Triple-Six

Anti
Against
Opposing

Cause
Man
Humanity

Strongest
Powerful
Greatest

Test
Caused
Triumphed

Won
All
Yesterday

Perfect Leader
Angry Man
Man of Reasons

Treasons
Faces (Many)
Identity

Treasured
Sought After
Known Evil

Antichrist
America
Person

3-6's
Animal

Beast

Armageddon
End Times
Apocalypse

End of the World
Numbered
Days

Counted
Lives
People

Games
Lives
Followers

All
Nations
Followers

Nations
World
Antichrist

USA
Everyone
Blindly

Few

Many
Forced

Smartest
Dumb
Realized

Works
Counted
Rewarded

Forgiveness
Sorry
Innocent

ID
Mad
Sorry

Identity
Bar-Coded
Mind

Controlled
Readings
Forceful

Brain
Forehead
Mind

Controlled
Purchased
Slavery

Triple-Six
Thoughts
Forced

One
Person
"Man"

Bible
Antichrist
"666"

Hell
Afterlife
Doomsday

Entrance
Eternal
"Satan"

Real
Official
Identity

Found-Out!
Realized
Defrauded

Decoded
World War III
Antichrist

One Man
America
USA

History
Living
Final Days

Judgment Day
Jesus On White Horse
Ending of Earth

Bad
Evil
Hell

God
Right
Heaven

USA
Riley Miller
Identity

Righteous
Heavenly

Angels

Rebellion
Satan
Heaven

Fought
Won
Fell

War
World
Three

Plus
Minus
Middle

Ours
Land
Everyone's

Free
Laws
Lands

Song
Dance
Rhythm

War

Treatises
Appointing

Minds
Body
Humanity

Personality
Classes
Hierarchy

The End
The Antichrist
The Apocalypse

WWIII
WWII
WWI

Happy
Flourishing
Better

Wins
Victory
Success

Black
White
Clearest

Forehead
Arm
Hand

666
One Man
Beast

Nothing
Clearness
Void

Darkness
Intelligence
Wonder

Light
Cave
Chains

No
Yes
Definite

Either
Or
Singular

Win
Lose
Void

Know
Think
Action

Tanks
Aircrafts
Boats

Jets
Pilots
Sailors

War
Declare
World

AC
USA
All

One
Nation
War

One
World
War

Repeat
3rd

War

Private
Public
Information

Economic
Government
People

Constitution
Bill of Rights
Emancipation Proclamation

Treatise
Documents
Handshakes

Church
Political
Speakers

Rules
Serves
Democracies

Worldwide
Wartimes
Three

President

Staff
Vice-President

Officials
Dignitaries
Magnates

Importance
Officially
Beneficial

Pro
Positive
Support

Life
Success
Gaining

Wars
Battles
Fights

Fright
Fears
Courage

Made
Decided
Attempt

"Pro"
"Con"
Declined

Jointly
Chiefs
Staff

Meeting
Gather
Socialite

Matters
Choices
Decisions

Walk
Fly
Ride

Strongest
Mind
IQ

Man
Person
Numbered

Decided
Chosen
Marked

Ordered
Newness
Worldly

I
WWIII
Light

Idea
Forehead
Number

Idol
Bible
Evil

Man
One
All

Evil
Good
Mark

Evil
Goodness
Liberty

Causes
Effects

Celebrated

Wars
Winning
Sides

Killing
Vision
Innocent

Murdered
Shot
Overpowered

Life
Persons
Allegiance

I
WWIII
AIC

Books
Manuals
Textbooks

Strongest
Smartest
Smarter

America

Russia
China

Survival
Contestant
Winner

Biblical
Antichrist
America

USA
Wins
Challenges

Presumption
Guessed
Factoid

USA
Wins
WWIII

Americans
WWIII's
Kills

Place
Date
Time

America
End Times
At Hand, The Hour Is

Evolution
Warfare
Survivors

Weakest
Strongest
Powerfulness

Kings
Nobility
President's

Soldiers
Fighting
Constructions

Remade
Pre-chosen
Fittest

Dallas
Santa Fe
Oxford

Texas
New Mexico's
England

Street
School
Independent

Smarts
Skills
Ability

Testing
Scoring
Learning

Perhaps
Maybe
Decidedly

Skillfully
Planning's
Masterful

Deadly
Alive
Living

Killed
Lifeless
Shot

Murdered
Killed

Assassinated

Laws
Rules
Legalities

Known
Popular
Famous

Readable
Plausibly
Scorings

Report
Documents
Treatise

Taken
Seized
Victorious

Class
Status
Report's

Social
Economic
Philanthropy

Hired

Recruited
Support

Earth
Planet
World

Decreed
Pronounced
Determined

Trains
Cars
Planes

Badness
Good
Reliable

Occupying
Seizing
Takeover

Terrain
Nature
Territory

Pride
Satisfaction
Agreeing

Homes
Offices
Workplace

Schools
Hospitals
Prisons

Lands
Freedoms
Democracy

Idealism
Fictional
Imagination

Party
Republican
Each

Party
Political
Past

Newness
Recruited
Followings

Ability
Purchase
Directedness

Belief
Life
Change

Old
New
War

Sold
Deformed
Tarnished

Lives
Hearts
Souls

Home
Work
Schooling

Three
Time-Span
Knowledge

Sided
Party
Slummed

Soldiers
Military

Fighters

Recipe
Information
Selections

Articles
News
Papers

Popularity
Gossip
Slander

Local
Distance
Nearby

Tops
High
Peak

Lands
Freedom
Fought

Smarts
Perfect
Skill

Targets

Groups
Grounds

Philosophy
Debate
Questions

Soldier
Kill
Save

Man
Antichristian
Human

Alive
Dead
Chosen

New World Order
Alliances
Old World Order

Banners
America's
Ownership

Saintly
Sinner
Freeing

Water
Food
Clothing

Adventure
Protective
Defending

Psyche
Atlas
Crazy

In Wars
Dialectical
Deranged

Promoting
Killings
Badges

Love
Neighbor
Peaceful

Attitude
Aggressive
Respect

Bodies
Training
Welfare

Pastors
Sermon
Death

Medals
Brave
Courage

Intelligence
Most
War-Times

Heroism
Activeness
Ranks

Plotting Points
Control Worlds
Decide Plans

Amazing
Structures
Capability

Winners
USA
Greatest

Duties
Saved

Lives

Great War
Unified
America

Glorified
Attributed
Adventures

Three Six's
One Person (Man)
Beware a Man

Duty
Active
Committed

Called
Service
Manhood

Holocaust
Relived
WW2 Of WW3

Predictions
Destruction
Humankinds

Visionary

Antichrist's
Following

Every Nation
The Triple-six
All Of Everyone

Warring
People
Following

The Antichrist
The Three Sixes
Mark On Forehead

Third World War
Freedom
American's A.C.

Win The USA
Over All The World
America Sole Nation

Everyone Following
Everything Controlled
Everybody Marked

USA President Obama
Watches Carefully
Role As Entire US

Killings Acts
Brotherhood Fighting
Soldiers Dying Forever

Washington, D.C.
Control Person's Desk
Presidential Control Point

Love Thy Neighbor
Birthed USA
Plan of Antichrist

Bombs Foreign Land
Attack Anti-American
Foreign Annihilation

USA's Whole World
Reconstruct USA
USA Wins Over All

The Club of Rome
The Societies of Places (USA)
The War Recruiting USA

War
Easy
Hard

Demands
Constructing
Buildings

Natures
Man
Animals

Rights
Places
Interest

Decisions
Leaders
Presidents

USA
Worlds
War

Warring
Level
Wins

Today
Now
This Moment

Wherein
Whatever
Wherever

Why Not?
Reasons

Causes

Wartimes
War Spots
War Places

Duty
Plans
Calling

Duty
Place
Things

Followings
Duties
Positions

Persons
Protect
Planet

Heard
Times
Productions

Times
Proclamations
Around World

News

Callings
Built

Persons
Duty
Called

Americans
Native USA
Productions

World War Three
Playing Fields
USA Citizens

Perchance
Directions
Aims

Spots
Protection
Hearsay

Gathering
Plans
Citizen

Build
Freedom
Plans

Democracy
Party
Republicans

Party
Followings
Reasons

Clubs
Societies
Memberships

Fellowships
Research
Willing

New Age World
The Order
New World Order

Persons
Places
Things

Events
Persons
Places

Chapter 5 –
The World I Made

Hard Times   American Wars
Useful Things   Society At Large
Philosophy Of War
States of USA   Places In World
Direction of War
Foreign Lands   Dire Needs of USA
Places of Plot
United States   Foreign Nations
Demand of Needs
Far Away Lands   Up-Close America
Places
United States   Russians
Foreigners
China   Germany
Localities
Allied Forces   United States of
America

USA WAR!
Third World War
Destined Into World
Will Come In Time – Due
USA Will Win Everything

Antichrist America!
To End The World – In War
World To Come – USA Victory
Prophesy In Bibles – End Times

Apocalypse – WWIII

World of Fear In America
Will Wipe Out Everything
Comes When America Ends

World War Plots!

Construction of a New America
Rebuilding of Roman Temple

USA'S Wars!

Supply and Demand For Goods
Resources of Needed Materials
Energy From Resources In USA!
Top Soldiers & Armies Brought To!

USA'S Peaces

The Generals and Presidents Protect
USA
The Men at War At Home Seek Good
The Supplies Are For War and Peace
The Peace of America Is At Home

American President

The Elected President Is For WWIII
The Vote For Office Makes Him Elect!
War for Him, Worked For Good
World War Three, Is Inevitable.

The War Effective

USA Is Homeland
Foreign Is Unprotected
Free Lands Are Good

The Peace Effected

Love is a Common Virtue.
Peace is not at all, of wars.
World Peace, is Impossible.

The Man In USA

We Make Our Own Choices.
At War, We Come Around.
The Man Is War-Based.

The Home War

The USA Is Protected!
No One, Can Destroy It!
America, Is Made To Be, Of Mine!

The Mind of America

Intellect
Mind
Imagination

Inspiration

Success
Life

All Three

USA Wars
USA Peace
World War III
Inspired Intellect
Freedom of Minds
The Reason Of Life As Too Much!

My Life

I, have habits. I, want to live, WW3.
I am depressed. I, do not love, life.
I have a reason. I am only a person.

WW3!

Soldiers

Payments
Satisfy
Home Front
War's A Nil
Impossible

Nothing
Something
Any Wars
No
Yes
Every War

Nations
Armies
World
War
Peaceful
Studied

Not
True
Biased
Fulfilled
Promising
Planning

Intellect
Machine
Superpower

Planning
Ideology
Americans

America
World
Third War
American
Gentile
Believers

Wars World Won

Pasts
Now
Kings
Won
Lost
Wartimes

Futures
Now Is How
President
Today
Purchases
Losses

Old USA
Kingdoms
USA Won
Emergency

Estranged
Topicality

New
Free
Won
Americans
Today
Alive
Fortune
Dealing
Empires

War's Won
Alliances
Newspapers
Pastimes
Present
Changed

The All-About America!
How America Wins WWIII!

Learning lessons, on killing.
Knowing America is innocent.
Trying hard, to know blamed.
To forgive, for tragedy.
To see the USA, in better ways.
Mistakes, are made to remake us.

Why Riley Miller Loses WWIII!

The Lost.
The Confused.
The Damned.
The Blamed.
War Calling.
War's Enemy.
WWIII Aliens.
World War Loser!

Lose Or Win?

Lost America, Means Nothing To Me.
Won America is, my life as good.

"USA'S WW3"

Feel Better.
Know Enemy.
Inspire Friends.
Counsel Brothers.
Win All Over.
Trusts In Oneself.
Treat People Well.
Seek First Good.
Correct No One.
Be a Happy Person!
Guard Your Mind!

An American Life!

Riley Miller's World View
Future President of USA
9-11's Deal
World Trade Center
Al Qaeda
Osama Bin Laden
Saddam Hussein
Terrorist Operations
Iraq and Iran War
Baghdad
ISIS Terrorist Group

Why, do we go to WW3?
The American Antichrist

How does American win?
Following The Antichrist To War

What is WWIII?
The Apocalypse of Armageddon

How is WW3 Fought?
Weapons of Mass Destruction of USA

Who Wins WW3?
America Wins

Why is it WW3?

The New World Order's Ending!

What does Christ do?
Rider on the White Horse

How WW3 Is Everyday?

Tomorrow
Everyone
Sundays
Everything
Everyday's
Each Day
All Days
New Days
Today
Living

WW3 Is Extinct!

Failure
Lost
Tries
Losses
Understanding
Damnation
Knowledge
Damned
Intelligent

Hell
Loss Days
Satan
Good Days
Hellishness
Peace

Life And Life's!

Pen
Hand
Sword
Side
Life
Deaths
Under
Armor
Pen
Side
Nail
Foot
Eyeballs
Contact Lenses
Forehead
Hat Brim
Head
Cowboy Hat

Death And Deals!

Sword
Sheath
Shot
Gun
Wound
Chest
Knife
Wastes

World War Three!

Expense
World Wars
Spending
Learning
Funding
Supportive
Lending
Participant
Sharing
Mutuality
Giving
Lending

(How Money Is Plan)

The USA'S Money!

Wealth of people in WW3

Poorest of those for WW3
Richest of loaners of WWIII
Paid highest of loot for WWIII
Surplus of money in WWIII
Lowest possible in WWIII
High earned dollar valued
Big expenses paid back to
No money earned for value
Giving money to World War

Money Meant Wars!

Richest Due to WW3
Least for WW3 In Support
Support through Loans to WW3
Highest Monetary Involved WW3
Most Support for WW3!
No Support from These People
Supported by Giving to Wars
No Show, No Dough in Wars
By Giving then Big Receiving

Big-Top From WW3's War!

Highest
Entertainment
Payments

Royalty

Payments
Dollars

Checks
Bill
Dollar

Big

Texas

USA

Pens

Signs

Signature

A Sealed Plan – WWIII'S USA!

Payments
Banks
Work
Spending
Cash
Accumulated Money
Big Earnings
Riches
Surplus

Money
Cash
Wealth
Banks
Fed
Office

The Lives Before War!!

Illuminati
Secret Plans
Hidden Agenda
Brotherhoods
Society
Groupings
Movements
Sealed Size
Measured
Republican
Democrat
Conservative
Predetermined
Ready
Sold

The Groups Movements To WW3

Secret
Public

Numerous
Heaven
American
Christian
Growing
Numbering
Larger
Books
Conspiracy
Theory
Mind
Clues
Sad

The Growing Movements To WW3!

Atomic
Nuclear
Biological
Racism
Anti-American
Selectivity
Foreign
Enemy
Holocaust
Bombs
Solders
USA Leads
One Man
One Country
One Enemy

Selective
Characters
Holy Bible
Global
Movements
Strength
Time
Life
Human
Evil
Good
Will
Power
Enemy
Love
Strive
Hardest
Anger
Big
Sizable
Grows
Spreads
Catches-On
Returns
Every
All
Tripled
Size

Height
Weight
Pro
Con
Null
Force
Power
Enemy
Home
Family
Sacred
Large
Big
Giant
Grows
Forward
Omniscience
End
Talking
Thinking
Dumb
Smart
Mighty

When WW3 Begins, What's?

Communications
Talking
Speaking
All Over

Every Corner
Each Side
Fast
Slowest
Beginnings
Starts
First
New
Fear
Love
Purpose
Shock
Killing
Hatred
Ability
Happy
Smiles
Impacting
Television
Friend
Sides
Choices
Willing
Knowledge
Commentary
Destruction
Frontal
Measured
Sizing
Judgment
Party

Related
Relativity
Evolution
Choices
Easiness
Frown
A-Bomb
Holocaust
Ends
Armageddon
"Hitler Man
Madman Leading
Questionable Life

World War III – Spreading Over
Already!

Soon
Afterwards
Deaths
Camps
Bases
Hidden Spots
Designated
Area
Designed
Walls
Assassins
Miller, Riley
Words

Picture
Internet
Social
Professional
Academic
Towns
Country
Democracy
Lives
Death
Talking
Roads
Bridges
Streets
Captured
Convict
Imprisoned
Life
Beings
Existing
Paths
Roads
Traveled
Peace
War
Already
Secret
Hidden
Unknown
Private
Rooms

House
Demonstrations
Christianity
Churched
Schedule
Events
Christians
Programs
Systems
Confinement
Education
Masses
Idealist
Fast
All
Limits
Story
Tales
Plots
Main
Big
Middle
Front
Lined
Proud
Business
Commerce
Gaining
Law
Order
NOA!

Song
Battle
Sing
Protect
Heard
Dear
Pro-Life
Guards
Cursed
Thrones
Crowned
Castles
Visionary
Product
Illuminated Ones
Weeds
Sicken
Weaken

NOA Or NWO – WWIII "OK"!

NOA
Age Movement
Same
Firstly
Last
3 Letters
King Making
New World Order
"NWO'S King"

NOA
New Order of the Ages
Novus Ordo Seclorum
N.W.O.
Latin
Tree
Family
Times
Old Age
New Ages
New Orders
Ordered
World
New
"Make Me King"
"As We Move"
Towards a "NWO"
Story
Battle
Prepare
Treatment
Royalty
New Aged Order
Places
Directions
Movements
Rules
Succeeds
Provides
Wealth
Abundance

Necessities
War
Living
Ruling
Strong
Loud
Silent
Proud
Big
Content
Product
Source
Provision
Transparent
Motionless
Motioning
Crowds
Personifying
Strongest
King
New
Order
Every
One
Thing
Not
Is
Isn't
Worth
Value
Rightness

Noteworthy
Practiced
Valuable
Against
Wills
Protagonist
War
Legion
Faction
Spiritual
Leadership
Foundation
Physical
Emotional
Intellectuals
Mistakes
Errors
Wrongs
Brains
Brawn
Know
Young
Prides
Values
Oldest
Aged
Order
Sciences
Physicality
Directions
Medications

Bandages
Syringes
War's
Peaceful
Times

The Road Less Traveled On-
That Has Made All The Difference!

Know
Sense
Awareness
Crowds
Biggest
Lives
Supporting
Holding
Building-Up
Partings
Eventually
Diverging
Challenges
Out Measurable
Willpowers
Parting
Ways
Separated
Differenced
Wayward
Directionally

Found
Support
Travels
Ending
Stopping
Point
Separated
Differenced
Wayward
Directionally
Found
Support
Travels
Ending
Stopping
Point
Separating
Learnable
Took
Less
More
Roads

The Roads To WWIII!

Firstly
Chosen
Arranged
Presumably
Guessed

Calculate
Know
Hire
Concerned
Ability
Trajectory
Target
Miserable
Calculated
Misleading
Found
Traded
Disclosed
Numbered
Calculated
Measured
Christian
Unbelievable
Faithful
Righteous
Considered
Valueless
Hard
High
Climb
Discovery
Agreeableness
Valuable

The Hard Way – To WWIII?

Antisocial
Unbelieving
Weakest
Strongly
Kinds
Prophetic
Knights
Darkened
Founded
Different
Divisions
Directed
Roads
Whole
Intersections
Lighted
Chosen
Left
Right
Wrongful
Directly
Alone
Woods
Divided
Destination
Unknowing
Evaluated
Choice
Proud

Rewarded
Paths
Straight
Unconformity
Story
Tale
Endings
Nuclear
Atomic
Weapons
America
Divisions
Straight
Forwards
Divided
Resumed
Repeated
Proclaim
Resounded
Valued
Limitless
Holocaust's
Desecration
Tragedy
Found-Out
Dead
Silence

The WWIII Stage!

Tanks
Guns
Soldiers
Ammunition
Infantry
Slaughtering
Killing
Graves
Losing
Rest
Death
Burials
Topics
Strangers
Personalities
Lives
Dreamt
Condemned
Lifelessness
Trail
Human
Directed
Founded
Saved
Dead
Alive
Harden
Souls
Ditched
Found Again

Rediscovered
Remade
Resounded
Limitless
Find
Lived
Became
Questioned
Unknown
War
Friends
Foes

What Repeats History?
Is WW3 Relived Again?

New Order
New World Order
New Aged Order
Ordered
Repeated
Aged Thrice
Tripled War
One World
Two Sides
Divided
Humungous
Separated
Allied

Joined
Good Sided
Evil
Opponents
Homeliness
Joint
Twice
Friends
Divided
Deaths
Orders
Divine
Wicked
Twofold
One World
Another World
Both "New" Ordered
Worldviews
Heroes
Villains
Gone
Won
USA
Alive
Dead
Found
Strength
Deaths
Godspeed!
Government
New World Order

Antichrist's WWIII
End Times
Biblical American's WW3
Governing Bodies
Dead USA Party
USA
Endings
Deaths
All of It
Dead and Gone
The End Is Near
History of Wars
Third War of Worlds
World War Three
Under USA Law
Be an American
Try WW3 American
Jesus Christ In WWIII
God the Father In Ending
The Church In Apocalypse
World War of NWO
History of WWIII to WW3!
The Military Genius of USA's!
The WWIII
The End of Creation in WW3!
The End of USA!
War Times in A.C.'S USA
The Loss of All Lives
The Lasting Endings Of Itself –
WW3 Intellect Is In Secret Societies

American Plans From Old Retold War
Lives
Remembering The History's Warred
Figures
Costing The Price To Pay, To Lives
Whom Lost
Comparing Presidential Books And War
Books, Of WWIII
Life And Death, To Wins Over WW3

To Try To Win! WW3!

USA
WW3
"A.C."
USA'S Antichrist One World
Sold to World Democracy
Bought By Final Offers
First One-World Government
Shadow Laws
One World Government
NOA
America's First Democracy
The Entire USA
All USA Followers of World
The New World Order
The Free World
Leader of Free World
Antichrist America

WWIII However, Is Dead at USA
Ending?

My Lesson In World War III –
The New World Order, Government!

Force of Real Law
Public Forces of Legalities
Private Function From NWO'S WWIII
The Party of the First Democracy
The Whole Worldwide Followers
Every Citizen Is Counted Included
Public Offices Serve Citizens
Governing Officials Served N.W.O.'S
WW3
Private Functions Relive WWII
The Government Is One-World-Order
The Followers Are From All Worlds
The Democracy Is Public Decisions
The A.C. Of One Man Is Represented
The Beast's Followers are False People
Heaven Fell Apart When A.C.'S WWIII
Is
Democracy Is Alive In USA
Follower's Party Agrees With New USA
Order
The USA's N.W.O. Hires One-World
Government
WW3 Presidential Office

Hired Office of WWIII – Govern World
Democracy
1-World Government/ NWO
Antichristian Life Head Towards
Presidential Endings

WWIII – "THE THIRD WORLD
WAR!"

What Riley Does In Wars, In How He
Hires The Office, Of Intention To Will
Into Power!
What Words, Are Written That Wills,
Wars Into Power? The President Of The
United States!

Riley Miller Of AMERICA!

From Riley Parker Miller –
A Bible Topic in My Holy Bible –

'Pride Promotes Strife

James 4 – 6
In NKJV Holy Bible

James 4 – 1

"Where do wars and fights come
From among you?
Do, they not come from your
Desires for *pleasure*,
That war in your members?

4 – 2

You lust and do not have.
You murder and covet and cannot
obtain.
You fight, and war.
Yet you do not have because you do not
ask.

4 – 3

You ask and do not receive,
Because you ask amiss,
That you may spend it on your pleasures.

4 – 4

Adulterers and Adulteresses!
Do you not know that friendship

With the world, is enmity with God?

Whoever therefore wants to be a
Friend of the world makes himself,
                An enemy of God.

                        4 – 5

Or do you think that the Scriptures,
    Says in vain, "The Spirit who
Dwells in us yearns jealously?"

                        4 – 6

                But He gives more grace.
                    Therefore He says:

                "God resists the proud,
        But gives grace to the humble."

Titus 2 – 14

Who gave Himself for us,
That He might redeem us
From every lawless deed
And purify for Himself
His own special people,
Zealous for good works.

From-
The Epistle of James

Jesus Christ In Bible's Verses –
The Holy Bible
The New King James Version!

The Writing Codex, Of The Book's
Protection From Biblical Codex, Came
From Out Of The Reader's Writing of
Words, Desired To Be From, What Is In
The Intelligent Designed Of The
System!

From The Ways Of Man! From What Is
In, This Written Style, On The Style, Of
The Books, From The President War
Office! The book's message, Therein
Lives Another Life, In The – "New
World Order!

Riley Miller Is The Approved
Contributor, To This Book, As The
Churched Prophet!

A Book Solely By – "Riley Parker
Miller!"

The History's Books

I Wrote Books, The Books Of the
History In Loving And Living
Everything In Life, To Its Greatest Form
– "Books Of The Best Quality", Never
Intelligence To Fail, And From Good
Teaching, Comes Knowledge, Inyo Easy
Books, Of Greatest, And Biggest, Then
Boldest, And Also Smartest, Books – I
Will Into Power! The Intelligence On
Books, As For The Easiest To Read, Into
Is The Library's History, Lives From
Houston, Texas, In To Of The Tiptop's
Of The World!!!"

The Highest Bear Order Of The AIC

The Highest Orders of the Beast
This is the Bear Order –
Welcome to World War Three's War On
The World In Countries Of The Living
Creature From The Bear!

The Holy Bible's - Riley Miller

www.ingramcontent.com/pod-product-compliance
Lightning Source LLC
Chambersburg PA
CBHW070752240726

48654CB00007B/48